5 Cool Ideas™
for Better Working, Living & Feeling

Cover & author photos by Don Kurek
Book design by Night Cry Graphics

Dedication

I want to thank five groups of people who have given me lots of Cool Ideas through the years.

First, I'd like to thank the Caruso family, including my parents Mickey and Ruth, who are still positive angels after all this time. My talented brothers, Joe, Rob and Dave continue to enrich my life, especially Webmaster Dave, who suggested that the Cool Ideas be stored in the kitchen fridge at EdisonHouse.com. My first ideas came to me in the presence of these exceptional individuals.

Second, I want to acknowledge my mentors, including Tom Deku and Joe Gilliam.

Third, I'd like to thank my associates and kindred spirits, including Dan Drotar, Jeff Jones, Polly Koenigsknecht, Don Kurek, Angie Marsh, Jim Pawlak, Duane Scherer, David Scherer and of course, lovely Sonya.

Fourth, I want to express appreciation to the thousands of students who have attended my keynotes, seminars and presentations. These people have contributed ideas in countless e-mails and phone calls.

Finally, thanks to my clients, who are a perpetual source of Cool Ideas. I'm especially grateful to customers who have hosted me for repeat visits, including Rayovac, Bank One, Citgo, the Barbados Ministry of Tourism, Hallmark and the United States Navy.

Table of Contents

Part II: Cool Ideas for Better Living (continued)

Part III: Cool Ideas for Better Feeling

Introduction

Some time ago, I started sending "5 Cool Ideas" to Edison House clients and prospects as a way of distributing good thoughts and developing new training topics. Feedback has been terrific! Over time, I accumulated quite a few topics and decided to bundle them together in a book.

The topics are grouped in three categories, represented by the three components of the Edison House logo. The "Better Working" category is symbolized by a light bulb. The "Better Living" topics are associated with a house and the "Better Feeling" category is represented by an exclamation mark.

This book can be enjoyed by reading from beginning to end, but you can also read a topic or a section at a time. Read topics in different seasons and at different phases in your life. Subsequent readings will almost certainly spark new ideas for you.

Visit www.EdisonHouse.com to keep up on the list of evolving topics, to receive regular installments of the series or to e-mail "5 Cool Ideas" to a friend.

I thrive on your success stories. Let me know what ideas work best for you. Send me a success story within 21 days. Suggest new topics and I'll add them to the next edition. E-mail me at 5CoolIdeas@EdisonHouse.com.

Michael Angelo Caruso
Royal Oak, Michigan

5 Cool Ideas™ for Better Working

5 Cool Ideas™
for Giving Killer Presentations

You make dozens of formal and informal presentations every day. Presentations can involve a large audience or a single person. Some presentations require large amounts of time, energy and money so you need to be efficient as well as impressive. Here are 5 Cool Ideas for giving killer presentations.

1 Effective openings make you impressive.

An effective opening sets the tone for positive results. Establish credibility by referencing a relevant statistic or a reputable literary source. I often begin seminars by saying, "This will be the best seminar you've ever attended." Audience members usually smile with delight, which is a desirable reaction to an effective opening.

2 Having fun is contagious.

Stories are fun. Tell stories. Make sure all stories have relevance or value. Fun stories offer a good ending with a moral or a lesson. Use humor but don't tell jokes. Announcing a joke puts too much pressure on the speaker to be funny and too much pressure on the audience to laugh.

3 Never lose sight of your goal.

A presentation is supposed to inform and incite. Ask yourself this question: What do I want the audience to do as a result of my presentation? All content should move listeners toward that goal.

4 Good handouts enrich the presentation.

Handouts are a terrific way to leave the audience with a part of you. Good handouts offer sources for more information and instructions for contacting the sponsoring organization. Include your phone number or web site address on each page of the handout.

5 Have a way to solicit feedback.

One easy way to solicit feedback is to stand by the door as people exit. Audience members will feel compelled to comment about your talk. Most of the feedback will be favorable because they are speaking directly to you. If you want constructive criticism, learn how to probe to the fifth level. You might ask questions like "What could I have done better? Why do you say that? What else could be improved? What do you mean by that? Who else can help me improve?"

5 Cool Ideas™
for Avoiding Information Overload

The good news is that we live in an information age. The bad news is that there seems to be way too much information. Here are 5 Cool Ideas for avoiding information overload.

1 Writing things down relieves stress.

Humans experience stress when they have to remember too much. Putting things on paper allows you to focus on more immediate concerns, like whether your zipper is down. Record the information into a time management system, rather than on scraps of paper.

2 Keep one calendar and put everything in it.

Maintain one calendar and keep it with you at all times. This calendar should include social events, work appointments and the kids' soccer games. Keeping one calendar will help integrate your business and personal life.

3 Use your planner as a diary.

Almost every time management system allows for daily journal entries. At the end of the month, these pages can be inserted into a binder that automatically becomes the easiest diary you can ever keep. A Personal Digital Assistant (PDA) can also help document your life.

4 Use e-mail to document your life.

Save important e-mail to topic folders labeled "Family" and "School." These time-stamped messages will serve as an official record of past events. At my company, the Edison House, we use e-mail messages as contracts, invoices and receipts. This cuts down on the amount of paper that needs to be filed and stored. Be sure to have a data backup in case your computer crashes.

5 You are what you read.

People who gossip, read junk magazines and watch bad TV will have richer lives when they choose not to process useless information. Try substituting magazine time with book reading. Instead of watching sitcoms, take in quality films. Remember, if you read good books and watch good movies and eat good food and drink good wine and think good thoughts and have good friends, you will have a good life. To read *5 Cool Ideas for a Good Life*, see page 96.

5 Cool Ideas™
for Finding a Mentor

Mentors can make your life a lot easier. Mentors and teachers have traveled a little further down life's road. They can tell you what to expect, give you ideas and introduce you to other mentors. Here are 5 Cool Ideas for finding a mentor.

1 People will help if you ask.

Concentrate on the end result rather than how you will find a mentor. Do you want another job? Do you want to meet someone in particular? Do you want to earn more money? Would you like work to be more rewarding? A mentor can help, but you will usually have to ask.

2 Everyone is a potential mentor.

Assemble your list of potential mentors without regard for whether they will say "yes." Possible mentors can include people who work at your company and people who don't. Consider listing men and women who work in other industries and other states. The people who run coaching websites say that most coaching is done via long-distance telephone line. Your mentor can even be a dead person. Benjamin Franklin has mentored me for years.

---

3   Honor a guru and they will honor you.

Pay your respects to potential mentors. Show concern for their biggest challenges. Ask them how they have been able to pass their knowledge and techniques to others. Tell potential mentors that you would be honored if they would help you. By paying your respects, you may earn the mentor's interest.

4   Mentors want you to be specific about goals.

Talk with potential mentors about specific goals rather than general plans. Mentors are busy and tend to be goal focused. If they decline to mentor you, politely thank them for their time and change the subject. If they say "yes," congratulations! You've found a mentor.

5   You might help the mentor.

The Law of Reciprocity states that if you do something nice for someone, they are likely to do something nice for you. While assisting the mentor, remind the person that you are still looking forward to learning from him or her. Help the mentor without any expectation of payback.

5 Cool Ideas™
for Providing Customer Service

The customer service industry is very competitive. Many products and services are indistinguishable. Excellent customer service can be the benefit that keeps your business alive. Your goal should be to develop what author Carl Sewell refers to as "customers for life." Here are 5 Cool Ideas for providing customer service.

1 **A Unique Selling Point sets you apart.**

Whether you market a product or service, you must find, cultivate and deliver a Unique Selling Point (USP). The USP is what distinguishes your product or service from the competition's. A Unique Selling Point can be a special feature or benefit. A USP can also be a slogan, a reputation or simply how you say "hello."

2 **Use peripheral listening to get true meaning.**

Try to understand what the customer is really saying by listening between their words. Some people refer to this technique as "peripheral listening." Peripheral listening is critical for improved customer service. An average waiter or waitress, for example, when asked about the ingredients of the soup, will simply tell you the ingredients. An exceptional server, however, will relay the ingredients and then try to discover why you inquired. They'll ask "Are you lactose intolerant?" and "Are you allergic to shellfish?"

3   Cliches do not make you distinctive.

Don't necessarily say and do what everyone else says and does. Just a little twist can help separate your offering from the rest of the competition. Cliches are boring and predictable. Cliches will help keep your product or service from being perceived as unique and distinct. Want to differentiate yourself from the competition? Instead of asking the customer "Can I help you?" ask "Do you know about our sale today?" Don't say "Have a nice day" when you can say, "I hope to see you again soon."

4   A customer's name is her favorite word.

Customer service is more impressive when it is personal. Personalize customer service with power phrases like "What can I help you with *right now?*" Use the customer's name when you hand back her credit card. Her name is her favorite word.

5   Continuous follow-up is good service.

After the transaction, use phone calls and e-mails to show the customer that you have unconditional positive regard for them. A phone call after the sale says "You were important to me when you were making the purchase and you're important to me now." This type of phone call can establish intense customer loyalty and generate tons of referrals.

5 Cool Ideas™
for Interviewing Prospective Employees

It's difficult to get good information about what applicants bring to the table. "Professional Interviewees" are exceptionally difficult to figure out. They have all the right answers and are initially very impressive candidates. Unqualified employees are nearly impossible to fire after they've been hired. The key to successful interviewing is to get the prospective employee to demonstrate desirable characteristics during the interview. Here are 5 Cool Ideas for better interview techniques.

1 Nonverbal responses say a lot.

Observe what candidates do as well as what they say. Neuro-linguistic programming (NLP) is the study of nonverbal communication. NLP, also known as body language, tells you everything you need to know about what someone is thinking. Remember the famous "Hmmm…" that asks, "Do you believe what people do or what they say?" To purchase my booklet, *Hmmm…Little Ideas with BIG Results*, visit www.EdisonHouse.com.

2 Get them to demonstrate what you desire.

If you ask job candidates if they are fun, most will say, "Yes." This doesn't mean they are. An East Coast transportation company drops a box of Legos in front of interviewees and watches their eyes. If candidates make a face, they're no fun. If they immediately smile and begin to build a model with moving parts and waterfalls, they are probably fun.

---

3   Unusual questions elicit honest answers.

Ask the candidate to name a favorite restaurant. Then ask him or her to direct you to the restaurant. You will quickly discover whether the person can give direction.

4   Creative techniques will garner new info.

Interviewers need to be creative in order obtain good information about the interviewee. Arrange for the candidate to demonstrate the desirable characteristic during the interview. If the job requires that the employee come to work on time, hold four short interviews instead of two long sessions. If the person can't tell you how to get to the restaurant from your office, he or she may offer to get back with you. If so, ask the candidate to call you the following day at 1:22 p.m. You will quickly find out if the person can take direction.

5   New info helps you make better decisions.

At the conclusion of the interview, thank the job candidate and suggest that the two of you go to lunch. Then, ask the candidate to drive. Observe nonverbal clues and immediately learn the answer to a question you cannot legally ask. In the United States, it is illegal to ask the interviewee if they own a car. In America, you may only ask if they have reliable transportation. Find new information during the interview and you will make better hiring decisions.

5 Cool Ideas™
for Being Professional

They don't teach it at colleges or universities. They don't teach it at most companies. Many business people do not have mentors to teach professionalism. Most people learn to be professional by trial and error. Here are 5 Cool Ideas for being professional.

1   Good information cancels bad information.

My friend and mentor Joe Gilliam says that professionals "need to take in new information." He's right. I process about 35 books every year. I read about 15 and I listen to the other 20. New positive information helps me cancel old, negative information. Consider that each of us has "negative angels" in our lives. Negative angels sit on your left shoulder and say things like "you can't do that" and "you're not good enough." Negative angels can be bosses, customers and even family members. Positive angels sit on your right shoulder and counterbalance the negative angels. Positive angels offer encouraging words like "you can do this" and "you have enough time." Published authors are positive angels that offer quality information.

2   Public service serves everyone.

Service work is the hallmark of a true professional. Rotary International, Optimist International and Big Brothers/Big Sisters are great organizations that can help you serve others. Dedicating time to those less fortunate and raising funds for important community projects is a great "give back." It's also one of the best ways to network.

---

3 Meet at least three new people per day.

Meet three new people every day and you will eventually build a network of terrific resources. Record your meetings in a data base because your contacts will eventually become your greatest asset. You can really enrich your network by making sure that you regularly introduce people in your network to each other. You can also use e-mail to do this. Simply send one person an e-mail and explain why that person should know the third party. Then include the third party's e-mail address in the "cc" function of the e-mail software.

4 Clothes are signals.

Your clothes say a lot about you. When you dress upscale, you send a signal that you are upwardly mobile and have self-respect. Clean, new clothes that are pressed and well coordinated assure others that you are professional, that you attend to detail and that you appreciate a certain standard. Dress a little better than those around you. Of course, flashy duds won't fool anyone if you don't communicate well.

5 Attend four seminars or speeches every year.

Polished speakers can be positive angels for you. When you regularly attend seminars, speeches and workshops, you will be exposed to other viewpoints and top quality ideas on how other professionals view the world. All of this can only help you become more professional.

5 Cool Ideas™
for Stronger Sales

Strong sales are the life blood of every thriving organization. Effective salespeople maintain contact with their sales network. Successful salespeople view rejection as temporary. They constantly work to uncover and deal with objections. Here are 5 Cool Ideas for stronger sales.

1 Network "five deep."

The idea is to network throughout the buyer's organization, making sure everyone knows how to reach you and why they should want to reach you. Communicate with the primary contact's immediate supervisor, an accounts payable representative, the purchasing agent and the primary contact's assistant.

2 Consistent contact is essential.

If your product or service is competitively priced, customers and prospects are likely to keep you on their vendor list. You will be removed from the list, however, if your contact with them is irregular or uncaring. According to the book, *Guerrilla Marketing*, by Jay Conrad Levinson and Seth Godin, 69% of dissatisfied customers leave due to inconsistent or nonexistent contact.

3 It's never "no," it's "no for now."

If a prospect refuses to purchase, do not consider this a rejection. In fact, a non-purchase is an opportunity to uncover an *ob*jection. If you can't close someone, odds are they can refer you to another prospect. Leverage the six degrees of separation by asking "Who do you know that would be interested in my product/service?"

4 Objections should be challenged.

Most sellers struggle when hearing comments like "I need more time to think about this" and "I'm not interested." Is the prospect unqualified or just veiling an objection? Ask bold questions to probe further. Ask in a soft "librarian tone" so you don't seem pushy. Say things like "It's interesting that you should say that. Please tell me why you need more time" and "I'm surprised that you're not interested." Act as if *not* doing business with you is the most unpredictable response you've ever heard.

5 Objections are opportunities.

First, test the objection to see if it is legitimate. Then, deal with the objection. Beware of "The Flinch," a common price objection that is usually a bluff. Remember that just because prospects object to the price, doesn't mean they are unwilling to pay that price. In a worst case scenario, price objections can be handled by trading value. "Our product is worth every penny, but if you'd like to pay less we can shorten your warranty." Strong sellers, of course, wouldn't advise prospects to shorten the warranty because it would discount the excellent value offered. In my sales training seminars, I teach sellers to have an answer to every conceivable objection. By thinking five moves ahead, sellers can use objections to move the prospect closer toward an affirmative decision.

5 Cool Ideas™
for Improved Writing

Elmore "Dutch" Leonard, is the author of more than three dozen books. Several of them have been made into motion pictures. Mr. Leonard, who happens to live a few miles from me, has published his rules of the writing game. He offers some terrific tips. Mr. Leonard's 5 Cool Ideas for better writing are in bold.

1 **"Avoid prologues."**

Life is short. Get on with it. Help your readers to do the same. Getting on with the story is also a great way to avoid writer's block. Launch right into the action and your writing will not stall in the "blank page" phase.

2 **"Never open a book with weather."**

For that matter, never open a memo with " . . . pursuant of our agreement." When writing, it's important to get to the good stuff right away. There'll be a good time to mention whether it's cloudy or sunny. There will never be a good time to be "pursuant of our agreement." While I'm thinking of it, use "daily" rather than "on a daily basis." There, I feel better.

3 **"Never use a verb other than 'said'…"**

"Never use a verb other than 'said' for dialogue," said Leonard. Sounds like more of a style preference to me, but the man is Elmore Leonard. He writes dialogue better than almost everybody. When writing

---

dialogue, try to write the exact way people talk. Use contractions and incomplete sentences, if appropriate. This is a great way to give dimension to your characters.

4 "... leave out the parts that readers skip."

Edit ruthlessly. Always try to say it in fewer sentences, with fewer words, using fewer syllables. Use a varied rhythm to discourage readers from skipping parts. Try a short sentence. Then, add a more complex sentence that includes an imbedded phrase or a combination of ideas.

5 "If it sounds like writing, rewrite it."

Rewrites rule! Always rewrite important e-mails, faxes and letters. They will improve every time you revise them. Speeches will benefit from rewrites, too.

5 Cool Ideas™
for Effective Outgoing Voicemail

Voicemail has become a way of life. Ever since Gordon Matthews invented the concept in the early 1980s, we've been looking for better ways to manage it, be creative with it and even circumvent it. Here are 5 Cool Ideas on how to make the most of your outgoing voicemail message.

1   Unique messages capture attention.

If you want people to think of you as special and distinct, don't use the same voicemail message that everyone else does. See if you recognize the verbiage in this trite message.

"Hello, this is John Doe. I'm not in right now, but your call is very important to me. Please leave your name and number at the tone and I'll get back to you as soon as I can." BEEP

2   Average people send average signals.

Sometimes, even a slight deviation from the standard recording can give your message all the distinction it needs. For example:

"Hi! This is John Doe with ABC Company and I appreciate your call. You can leave your message now." BEEP

3   Tease callers and they'll join in.

Many people employ a unique "teaser" in their outgoing voicemail message. This version teases the caller into inquiring about your "awesome day."

"Hi! This is John Doe. Today is July 24 and I'm having an awesome day. Please leave your message after the tone." BEEP

4 Your message should match your mission.

Voicemail greetings work best when they match the company's mission (i.e., innovative), corporate culture (i.e., creative) or the individual's personality (i.e., energetic).

"Hi, it's John with ABC Company. According to my horoscope, I am going to hear from some nice people today. Thanks for calling. I'll get right back with you." BEEP

Insert bits of your corporate mission statement into your outgoing message. Recite your personal creed. Revel or despair about the score to a recent football game. Offer a movie or book endorsement. Sing a couplet from a popular song. Make birthday announcements. Have fun!

5 Confidence attracts competence.

Confident outgoing voicemail messages suggest a high level of customer service. Of course, you are obligated to follow through on everything you suggest.

"Hi! You've reached John Doe with ABC Company. Please leave a message of any length and I will call you back within the hour." BEEP

Remember, the key is to be distinctive without being ostentatious. Be functional without being routine. Find my phone number at www.EdisonHouse.com and call to hear my unique, distinctive, confident voicemail message.

5 Cool Ideas™
for Efficient E-Mail

At its best, e-mail is inexpensive and convenient. At its worst, e-mail can be overwhelming and inefficient. Here are 5 Cool Ideas for making e-mail more efficient.

1 Make the "subject line" specific.

The "subject line" of an e-mail is a terrific opportunity to summarize the essence of your message. Avoid putting vague phrase like "Hi, Mike" in the subject line. If the mail includes important information, don't type "Meeting Update" when you need to convey "Tuesday's Meeting is canceled." If the message is time sensitive, write "Please reply by Friday, October 10." Using fully-capitalized words, whether in the subject line or the body of the letter, is considered "shouting." Shouting is bad etiquette.

2 An organized mailbox is a happy mailbox.

Learn how to search your computer to find e-mails by sender, date, subject and key words. Also, you might want to save certain e-mails to files labeled "House Purchase" or "Surgery." Finally, when replying to a long message, delete the parts of the original missive that aren't applicable.

3   Review important messages before sending.

Queue critical messages to send at a later time. Give yourself at least a half-day to improve and approve your verbiage. Then, carefully proofread the document to make sure you're using the exact words necessary. Reading aloud is a great proofreading technique. Run a spelling and grammar check before sending.

4   Use a signature file to make e-mails distinct.

Your signature file should include information about how to contact you. Provide telephone area codes and complete URL addresses (with "http://www.") so that readers can point and click. See page 28 for *5 Cool Ideas for Your E-mail Signature File.*

5   E-mail is a one-way form of communication.

E-mail is convenient, but it's a one-way form of messaging. If you send a message and a few days pass with no response, resend the message with this additional note: "I'm not sure my e-mail is working properly. Did you receive my message three days ago?" Be sure to reference the original subject line. You might also include the words "second request" in the subject line. If you still don't receive a reply, call them or go visit.

5 Cool Ideas™
for Your E-mail Signature File

E-mail signature files are an opportunity to leave an important impression with readers. An e-mail "sig file" is a chunk of text that always appears at the end of your outgoing e-mail messages. You can easily arrange for your computer to automatically tag a signature file at the end of every e-mail you send. Here are 5 Cool Ideas for your e-mail signature file.

1 Signature files are miniature messages.

Think of your e-mail signature file as an electronic elevator speech. See page 108 for *5 Cool Ideas for Your Elevator Speech.* The little blurb at the end of your e-mails can say a lot about who you are, what you offer and what you want. Use your signature file to inspire, clarify and entertain your readers. Change it often to reflect your dynamic personality. Leave it the same and bore people to death. Always use a brief signature file.

2 Be unique and be regarded as unique.

Your sig file should be more than just your name, rank and serial number. A good signature file conveys your personality by using words to reflect your passion. Show readers you're human by offering a favorite quote, relaying a song lyric or conveying a bit of your corporate mission statement. Make your message unique and people are more likely to perceive you as unique. Remember, distinct business people usually have more value than non-distinct business people.

---

3   Send a message with your signature file.

If you're selling something, the sig file can promote the product or service. Display a little of your personal and corporate philosophy by pledging a specific quality of customer care like "I return all calls within 24 hours." Make good on your pledge. If appropriate, notify readers when you're leaving and returning from vacation.

4   Keep a folder of favorite sig files.

Some things are worth repeating. For years, I've kept a folder of my best signature files. They include holiday greetings, birthday announcements, cool quotes and clever couplets. I reuse my favorite sig files.

5   Encourage readers to respond.

The best electronic elevator speeches provide info for readers to contact you. Include all contact info, such as your full name, company name, business address, phone number with area code, fax number, cell phone number and the best times to reach you. For a sample of my current signature file, e-mail me at MichaelCaruso@EdisonHouse.com. Put "sig file" in the subject line.

5 Cool Ideas™
for Icebreakers at Meetings

Physically, it can be easy to bring people together, but arranging an intellectual interface can be challenging. Here are 5 Cool Ideas to help people interact during meetings. You can find detailed steps for each activity at EdisonHouse.com.

1 The "Paper Tear Game" opens perspectives.

This simple activity helps participants understand that even the simplest task is open to interpretation. Managers can use this exercise to effectively defend themselves when subordinates claim "Your directions weren't clear." The Paper Tear exercise teaches people to think for themselves and to ask clarifying questions. **Group size:** 2 to 200 people. **Props:** an identical piece of paper for all participants. **Time:** 5 minutes.

2 A "Round Robin" helps people loosen up.

The Round Robin is an excellent way to get people to loosen up and enjoy a meeting. The facilitator should give participants five minutes to find something they like about two people in the room. After five minutes, the participants return to their seats. The facilitator begins the Round Robin by asking one of the attendees to introduce another participant and say something positive. Then the person introduced does the same for another person and so on. **Group size:** 10 to 25 people. **Props:** none. **Time:** 10 minutes.

3 "Don't Drop the Customer" builds teams.

This game is excellent for teaching groups the value of teamwork. It also reinforces positive behavior, encourages communication and rewards people for efficiently solving problems. Have everyone stand in a large circle. In this game, everyone has an in-box and an out-box. The out-box is represented by a person around the circle. One cannot be next to one's in-box or out-box. Announce that "everyone must touch the customer." The most important goal is to not drop the customer. The game is repeated several times as "management" evaluates the results with funny and educational comments. **Group size:** 15 to 40 people. **Props:** an empty water bottle, a table cloth and a mint. **Time:** 15 minutes.

4 The "Listening Exercise" helps folks focus.

This terrific little exercise helps people practice their listening skills in unexpected ways. The facilitator has the attendees pair off and sit "kneecap-to-kneecap and eyeball-to-eyeball." One person is the Listener and one person is the Speaker. The Listener maintains eye contact with the Speaker and does not respond verbally. The Speaker also maintains eye contact and talks about any topic for three minutes. Eventually, the roles are reversed. **Group size:** 6 to 60 people. **Props:** movable chairs for all participants. **Time:** 10 minutes, including an "afterglow."

5 Thinking about success is the first step.

The objective of this icebreaker is to get participants to pledge specific improvement regarding their job. Ask attendees to write this phrase: "I could be more successful, if I _____." Another version is: "I could be happier, if I _____." The facilitator helps the participants create a master list of words that could fill in the blank, i.e., more confident, more educated, more self-assured, better listener, less emotional, less angry, etc. Participants are then asked to fill in their blank with what they would like to improve, thereby predisposing themselves to this topic during the meeting and all but pledging personal improvement. **Group size:** 3 to 3,000 people. **Props:** none. **Time:** 15 minutes.

5 Cool Ideas™
for Firing Someone

Firing an employee is usually an uncomfortable event for everyone involved. Melodrama and damaged egos can make a mess of the proceedings if you don't use these 5 Cool Ideas for firing someone.

1 Avoid using the "F" word.

Instead of telling someone you're going to fire them, tell them you're encouraging "career redirection." We're all on our way someplace else and while being fired seems lonely and final, a career transition hints of hope and a vocational upgrade.

2 Encourage the employee to take another job.

In most employment termination situations, the employee isn't enjoying the relationship any more than you are. Appeal to his or her common values. Encourage the employee to consider working in another department, at another company or in another industry. Plant the seed of change by asking "What's your dream job?" and following up with "You should never give up on your dream job." In a soft tone add, "You deserve to be happy, don't you?" Then, change the subject. Casually mention the conversation later to underscore your sincerity and drive home your message.

---

3   Give employees permission to move on.
Unhappy, unproductive employees stay at jobs for a variety of reasons. Some people stay because they believe quitting is an unacceptable solution. Convinced that if they don't quit, they won't be a failure, employees will spend 20 years with a company they don't like. Give employees permission to quit by helping them understand the big picture.

4   Arrange for employees to quit.
Problem employees can be psychologically moved closer to the exit door by physically moving their work station. It's true that a manager cannot penalize a chronically absent employee as long as the employee proves that a doctor has ordered him to stay home. Managers can, however, move the absent employee's work station in order to improve departmental efficiency. When the absent employee returns to work and can't find his desk, the manager will definitely have the employee's attention. Techniques like this can make an employee uncomfortable enough to improve his attendance or quit.

5   Be an advocate, not an adversary.
Offer to give the problem employee help in finding another job. You're not committing to job placement, just offering to give whatever assistance you can, including moral support. In *The 21 Irrefutable Laws of Teamwork*, John Maxwell writes that your team's weak link deserves to be a strong link on another team.

5 Cool Ideas™
for Dealing With
Entitlement-Based Employees

Entitlement-based behavior can certainly make work life unpleasant. Entitlement-based employees often believe that the company exists to serve them. They are known for working to a minimum standard and usually don't volunteer for any extra duties. Here are 5 Cool Ideas for dealing with entitlement-based employees.

1 Their past can be helpful in the future.

Entitlement-based employees learned their attitude at home or at prior jobs. You can't change their outlook, but you can provide information that may influence employees to modify their attitude, which could result in improved behavior. Casually inquire about the employee's background and past imprinting. Avoid making an inquisition. Ask questions like "What did your father do for a living?" and "What's your earliest memory?" Make it clear that this information is "off the record" and that you are not interested in judging them. Offer comparable tidbits about yourself, even if the entitlement-based employee doesn't ask.

2 Finding rewards requires patience.

Find innovative and fun ways to remind entitlement-based employees how talented they are. Offer positive reinforcement such as personal compliments, gift certificates, time off and cash bonuses. Try different combinations of awards. Be patient as you identify awards that motivate.

---

3   Education can temper entitlement.

Help entitlement-based employees link behavior
modification to reward. Remember to let them tell
you what the appropriate reward is. Send the employee to seminars and give them a tour of the
company's resource library. Refer them to Stephen
Covey's *The 7 Habits of Highly Effective People*,
which highlights the wonderful merits of interdepen-
dency. Show them the value of being free of the
entitlement mindset. Use specific examples of
their behavior, if you can do it without rankling.

4   Good role models influence others.

Demonstrate the attributes of a committed, integrated
employee. Rather than preach or showboat, casually
display the personal benefits of a non-entitlement
mindset. Continually invite the entitlement-based employee to participate with you next time.

5   Raising the bar raises performance.

During my seminars, I am often asked how to deal
with entitlement-based employees who find so much
time for personal telephone calls, internet surfing and
office chitchat. The solution is to raise the productivity bar. Hold the employees to a higher standard
by making them accountable for their time. Use re-
ward/consequence proposals to encourage desirable
behavior. See page 138 for *5 Cool Ideas for Creating
Reward/Consequence Proposals*.

5 Cool Ideas™
for Working a Room

Lots of people are good networkers, but few know how to work a room. Making social contacts at a cocktail party or business reception is a skill that requires conversational dexterity, consistent discipline and a desire for detail. When you know how to work a room, you will make more connections, do more business and be liked by more people. Do it wrong and you could be perceived as brash, catty and undesirable. Here are 5 Cool Ideas for working a room.

1 Work the parking lot for fun and profit.

When working a room, there's no need to warm up. Start making connections as you walk through the parking lot. After all, anyone who parks where you do might be attending the same function, right? Well, these nice strangers are attending the event so they can meet people like you. Work the lot, the foyer and the coat room line. Use verbiage like "Are you excited about this event?" and "Have you met anyone interesting so far?" to break the ice with your new friend. Work the foyer on the way out, too.

2 Use every opportunity to shake hands.

People are your greatest resource, so initiate conversation. Commit to meeting as many people as possible in the first 15 minutes of the event. Hold out your hand and introduce yourself to everyone who walks toward you. Avoid the temptation to hunker with someone at the bar or in the corner of the room. You can always return to the most interesting people later.

---

3   Networking is about them, not you.

Make it a point to focus the conversation on the other person. Plan several topics in advance so that you're not at a loss for subject matter. Keep the topics positive and upbeat. Avoid negative comments about other people and don't talk about unpleasant current events. Ask open questions that encourage others to talk about themselves and their interests. Be generous and thoughtful about introducing people to each other. Always compliment people as you introduce them. Use first names, if you can't remember full names. If you struggle to remember a particular name, softly ask the person her name and then give it to the third party. See page 66 for *5 Cool Ideas for Remembering Names*.

4   Have several elevator speeches available.

When it's time for you to answer questions about yourself, choose an appropriate "elevator speech" to make a strong impression. Be brief, upbeat and original when you talk about yourself. See page 108 for *5 Cool Ideas for Your Elevator Speech*.

5   Follow up with an "urge to action."

As you work the room, collect business cards and literature from everyone you meet. In a quiet moment, write a quick note on each card to remind you of what you can do for the person or what they might do for you. Record what you talked about so that you can follow up with them within 48 hours. The more detailed your notes, the easier it will be to impress the person when they receive your follow up message.

5 Cool Ideas™
for Promoting Seminars

Learning is most fun and most effective when it is easy and natural. Yet, the very nature of seminars and other classroom activities sometimes makes people uptight and anxious. "Seminar resistant" people pose a challenge for seminar promoters and seminar leaders. Here are 5 Cool Ideas for effectively promoting seminars.

1 Strategic language can sell the event.
There's a bit of Hollywood in the seminar business. Refer to the speaker as a "special guest speaker." Refer to the activity as an "event" rather than a "seminar." You can also refer to it as a "show." If your seminar presenter can't deliver a show, get another presenter.

2 Mandatory events can create problems.
If you make the event "mandatory," you risk alienating people who feel that the program is being forced on them. Instead, establish positive expectations for attendees using phrases like "you will never forget this program," "this will be the best seminar you have ever attended" and "you will directly benefit from this program within 24 hours of attending."

3 A big event creates a big buzz.
Promote the training as you would a concert. Arrange for the speaker to be interviewed by a reporter with the local newspaper and the host of local talk radio program. Publish the speaker's credentials in your corporate newsletter. Print tickets to the "main

event." Invite special guests like favorite customers, vendors and local dignitaries. Have a special reception prior to the program to create even more buzz.

4 Make part of the event "exclusive."

This marketing technique creates desire in "seminar resistant" people. Schedule special receptions or meetings for certain departments or pay grades. Refer to that portion of the event as "invitation only" and later open it to everyone if you'd like. Remember the psychology axiom that states, "People tend to want what they cannot have."

5 Use the event to promote future training.

Solicit verbal and written evaluations. Be sure that evaluation forms have a narrative section at the top to capture specific comments. Notify attendees that they are required to submit a paragraph summary of what they learned. Instruct attendees to include a written pledge to apply one seminar idea in their day-to-day routine. Make sure everyone knows you will ask them how the application of the idea has improved their quality of work. Ask them at their next performance review. The paragraph summary links the employee's commitment to their performance and their performance to their review, making your training more relevant and more effective.

5 Cool Ideas™
for Keynoting

Keynotes are usually short speeches that are delivered during a formal meal. Keynote speeches are challenging to deliver because of all the distractions. Silverware is clanking and servers are flitting about the room. Often, keynotes are positioned at the beginning of a conference, which requires the keynote speaker to set the tone for the entire event. In any case, the keynoter's task is to formulate and convey the meeting's main message. Here are 5 Cool Ideas for delivering powerful keynotes.

1 Visit the room before you speak.

When you visit the room prior to the speech, sit in different chairs to get a view of the podium or speaker platform. Imagine people entering the room and taking their seats. Imagine yourself visiting the various tables prior to the speech, introducing yourself to members of the audience. Test your microphone before people enter the room. Arrange to have the audiovisual expert and a representative of the facility available at the start of the keynote in case there are any technical snafus. These simple exercises will make the room familiar and friendly.

2 Editing will strengthen your speech.

Keynotes last 20-40 minutes, so you've got to make your message efficient. The general formula is to present your thesis statement, give several examples or stories to support your thesis and then summarize. Write and rewrite your speech. Edit ruthlessly.

---

3   Teach something in the first four minutes.

Use the first four minutes of a keynote speech to thank the person who introduced you, personally address the honored guests and teach the audience something they don't know. All of the above will validate your professionalism at the beginning of your speech when you need it most. By the way, an effective introduction by your host can teach the audience something about you and the topic before you even begin speaking. Prior to the speech, visit with the person who is introducing you. Review the introduction and exactly what they should say. Do this even if you sent the intro to them in advance.

4   Tell stories that teach lessons.

Make sure all your signature stories have relevance, value and a unique positive message. See page 132, for *5 Cool Ideas for Your Signature Story.*

5   Urge the audience to take action.

Use a strong close that urges the audience to take action. Ask this question of the speech: What do you want the audience to do as a result of your keynote? Do you want them to attend an event? Donate money? Do something before Saturday? Whatever you want them to do, leave them with the next step for doing it. When audience members take that step, you'll know you delivered a strong keynote and people will invite you to do more public speaking. See *5 Cool Ideas for Improved Public Speaking* on page 56.

5 Cool Ideas™
for Becoming a Speaker

Through the years, I've helped many people get started in the speaking business. Here are the 5 coolest ideas I have for becoming a public speaker.

1   Every gathering is a speaking opportunity.
Start speaking now. Speak everywhere. Speak in your doctor's waiting room and on crowded elevators. Don't be weird about this. Get used to engaging people in a variety of settings. Be the voice that toasts and the first person to ask questions in a group setting.

2   Learn to enjoy the willies.
Are you nervous when speaking? Dale Carnegie said that the only way to get used to something is to do it often. After a while, your system will adjust and speaking won't be quite so challenging for you. The willies might never go away, but you can eventually get used to them.

3   Listen to lots of speakers.
Attend lots of speeches and analyze them in audio format. Pay attention to personal styles and techniques that seem to work. Don't copy other speakers. Instead, try to adapt your own style. Study the masters, in person and on audiotape or videotape. I recommend Zig Ziglar, Terry Sjodin, Brian Tracy, Les Brown, Gail Cohen and Roger Dawson. Listen for tone, cadence, volume, pitch and the space between the words.

---

4 Live for networking.

Get your name out there in every possible way. Start a data base. Collect business cards from everyone you meet. Develop a "hit list" of influential people that you want to know and people that should want to know you. Do the same with the big shots in the speaking business. Use your database to send periodic messages that offer value-added information about how your speaking skills can serve them. See *5 Cool Ideas for Building Better Relationships* on page 64.

5 Three revenue streams are available to you.

Start thinking ahead. Good speakers are good because they have something worth saying. Most things worth saying are worth writing and some things worth writing are worth publishing. Speakers who are published authors have more credibility and in general get paid more for their speeches. Dottie Walters, author of *Triple Your Income*, recommends speaking to sell your writing and writing to sell your speaking. She also suggests that you use your speaking and writing to sell your consulting services.

5 Cool Ideas™
for Motivational Job Descriptions

Job descriptions are commonly used to hold employees accountable to a performance standard. Most job descriptions are demotivating because they are employer-friendly. The documents are written in general, subjective language that includes one-way phrases like "other duties as assigned." The job description might generally suggest that the employee should greet the customer, but does not specify that the employee should smile when greeting the customer. Since employees have little to no ownership in job descriptions, they usually have no buy-in. When you create job expectations with the employee, the employee will more likely feel responsible. Your Human Resource department will not have a problem with this technique as long as you leave the job description in place. When dealing with employees, simply refer to their job expectations rather than their job description.

1 Reward is a motivator.

Mention the vague and general job description to the employee. Explain that a specific list of job expectations will give her greater clarity about her job responsibilities and will allow you to reward her more appropriately. The employee will likely buy into the reward concept. This buy-in is imperative.

2 Get the employee involved in the process.

Ask the employee to list their specific job duties. This may take a while. No matter what is on the list, thank the employee for creating it and compliment them on some aspect of the document.

3 Specific expectations serve everyone.

Go through the list with the employee making the expectations specific. For example, the employee might list "greeting the customer" as a job expectation. Remind the employee that "greeting the customer" is vague and general and that the job expectations are to be specific and focused. Have her add "smile within 30 seconds of greeting the customer," if you'd like. Likewise, the non-specific job descriptor "answer the phone" will become the specific job expectation "answer the phone within two rings."

4 "Living documents" perpetuate new ideas.

In order to link the job expectations to reward, it's a good idea to get a copy of the job expectations into the employee's personnel record as a "living document." Union and government protocol may only allow the document into the personnel file as "discussion notes," which must be purged after a few weeks. In any case, employees are more likely to honor their job expectations than their job descriptions. After all, they inherited their job description, but they helped create their job expectations, which are in their handwriting.

5 Link expectations to performance reviews.

Tell the employee that she will receive the highest possible review if she performs to the highest possible job expectation. The key is to not make the employee wait a long time for her performance review. Use the narrative section of the performance evaluation form to show your appreciation. See *5 Cool Ideas for Motivational Performance Reviews* on page 46.

5 Cool Ideas™
for Motivational
Performance Reviews

Most performance reviews are demotivating because they are given only once a year. Using vague and subjective job descriptions as a performance standard, demotivating reviews tend to focus on the past, which the employee can't change. Demotivating reviews often position the employee as a passive guest to the process. A performance interview, however, is an effective motivational process because it occurs several times annually. Using specific job expectations as a performance standard, interviews keep employees involved and interested in their future. Here are 5 Cool Ideas for making performance reviews motivational and effective.

1   Quarterly interviews are motivational.

Your Human Resources department will be okay with performance *interviews* as long as you keep the performance review in place. The annual review tends to be tied to the employee's anniversary date and raise. Enjoy a one-on-one meeting with the employee every 90 days. Refer to the meetings as "performance *interviews.*" The quarterly interview should be upbeat and not tied to money. Interview your employees quarterly or they will interview someplace else.

2   Job descriptions are not motivational.

Most job descriptions are general and employer-friendly. It's better for managers to reference "job expectations," a list of specific duties employees create with their manager. Page 44 has *5 Cool Ideas for Motivational Job Descriptions*, which outline the merits of motivational job expectations.

3   The past is not as motivational as the future.

Managers usually use performance reviews to talk about the past. This is demotivating because the past can't be changed. Quarterly *interviews* reference the future, specifically the next three months. Ask the employee what specific plans they have to honor their job expectations and career goals during the next 90 days.

4   Offer no criticism at performance interviews.

Ask the employee "What do you like most about your job?" and "How can I get you more of what you like?" Deliver no criticism at the performance interview. Give constructive criticism during the year as needed.

5   Let the employee tend their own career.

In most cases, managers are doing too much work regarding performance reviews. The employee should look after his or her own career. Encourage the employee to prepare, chair and summarize their own performance interview. Smart managers will ask the employee to schedule his or her own interview, ensuring that the manager will never be late in scheduling another employee performance meeting.

5 Cool Ideas™
for Motivational
Performance Evaluation Forms

Most performance evaluation forms have a numerical section and a narrative section. These evaluations can be demotivating because the company focuses on the numerical portion of the evaluation, while the narrative portion is the most important to the employee. Another problem is that pay raises are tied to the numerical ratings, but most middle managers are not authorized to give pay raises. Here are 5 Cool Ideas for evaluation forms that motivate.

1   Link job expectations to the eval form.

If you establish a direct link between employees' job expectations and their reward for performing to those expectations, most employees will be motivated to comply. If, however, employees are unsure or unclear about whether to answer the phone within two rings or smile within 30 seconds of greeting the customer, they are sure to be disappointed when reading their performance evaluation form. See page 44 for *5 Cool Ideas for Motivational Job Descriptions*, which teaches the concept of job expectations.

2   Fill out the evaluation forms quarterly.

We know that filing annual performance evaluation forms does not motivate employees as much as when we fill out the forms quarterly. See page 46 for *5 Cool Ideas for Motivational Performance Reviews*.

---

3   Reward "5" work with "5" ratings.

Managers send mixed signals when they reward superior work with less than superior ratings. When a "5" is a superior rating, managers sometimes say things like "I never give all 5s," and "There's always room for improvement." When employees hear this, they feel confused and betrayed because they can never receive the highest score. This demotivates the employee and damages the credibility of the manager.

4   Use narratives to provide deep compliments.

In his seminal work, *The 7 Habits of Highly Effective People*, Dr. Stephen Covey writes that strong compliments or "emotional bank deposits" are the fastest way to build rapport with people. Smart managers and supervisors use the narrative section of the performance evaluation form to deliver strong emotional deposits like *"I really appreciate that you are never late for anything"* and *"I'm really glad you're on my team."*

5   Individual reward should not be relative.

It is demotivating to rate individual performance relative to the performance of other workers. Most managers are only authorized to give a certain number of "5s," regardless of how the individual employee performs. In some cases, managers ration "5" ratings because a superior rating would indicate that the employee is entitled to a raise. Since it is financially impossible to give everyone a raise, only those who get more money will receive a superior performance evaluation form. Of course, employees want to receive "5s" on their evaluation form whether they receive a pay increase or not.

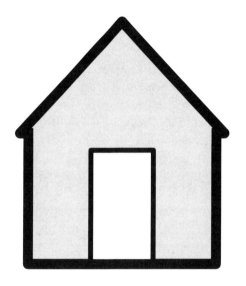

5 Cool Ideas™ for Better Living

5 Cool Ideas™
on How to Be More Attractive

If being physically attractive means to be good look-ing on the outside, being psychologically attractive is to be good looking on the inside. Being psycho-logically attractive is a talent that is helpful in al-most any line of work and certainly useful in per-sonal life. Here are 5 Cool Ideas on how to be more attractive.

1 It is good to be "attractive" on the inside.

In America, we tend to think of attractiveness as be-ing young, sexy and pretty. By that definition, when we are no longer young, we are no longer attractive. Let's think of it another way. The root word of at-tractive is "attract" and we are trying to attract our greatest resource – other people.

2 Your unique qualities are attractive.

In his fantastic book, *The Four Agreements*, Miguel Ruiz writes that we often compare ourselves to an image of perfection in order to be accepted. When we discover we are not perfect (which for me hap-pens every day), we reject ourselves and send sig-nals to others that we are not good enough. The art of being attractive helps you focus on what you have to offer. When you display your unique and special characteristics to others, they will not only accept you, they will be attracted to you.

3   Show and tell people how you are special.

Develop an "elevator speech" that can be delivered to people that you meet. This short speech will allow others to get excited about you and help them anticipate interaction with you. Deliver your message in exciting, provocative sound bites. For instance, instead of saying "I'm a teacher," smile and say "I mentor heroes." Instead of saying "I work in a child care center," jut out your chest and say "I create memories." Avoid clichés. Focus on leaving distinct, positive impressions. See page 108 for *5 Cool Ideas for Your Elevator Speech.*

4   Everyone is an expert at something.

Position yourself as an expert. Write a 500-word essay. Submit it to your corporate newsletter office. Send it to your favorite trade publication and your local newspaper. Create a twenty-minute presentation and arrange to deliver it to local Rotary and Optimist clubs at lunchtime. You will be sowing seeds from which great things will grow.

5   Find others to be attractive.

By acknowledging the attractiveness of others, you will undoubtedly become very attractive yourself.

5 Cool Ideas™
for Safer Travel

I once had a laptop computer stolen from my hotel room. Investigators discovered that the door to my room had been opened three times while I was out eating dinner. The key that was used had been issued to a person who worked at the hotel. The hotel asked me to prove the computer had been stolen. Of course, I couldn't. Discomfort and danger await the unprepared traveler. You can help guarantee that your trips are safe and worry free with these 5 Cool Ideas for safer travel.

1 Keep a low profile when traveling.

If the hotel desk clerk announces your room number when you check in, hand the key back and ask the clerk to assign another room without saying the number aloud. Never ask for restaurant directions when checking into a hotel. People in the lobby might overhear these conversations and gain knowledge that would compromise your privacy and safety.

2 Be aware of laws that protect others.

Never leave anything of value in your room. Pass keys are everywhere and the hotel will not usually be liable for theft. One hotel-friendly law is commonly referred to as the "Innkeeper Statute." Some version of this statute is posted on the door of most hotel rooms. This law states that if someone steals a computer or a wedding ring from your room, the hotel is only liable for a relatively small dollar amount – in most cases, about $200.

---

3 Lock your stuff even when it is "safe."

Strange as it seems, people will lock up a $400 bike if they go into an ice cream parlor, but they won't lock a $4,000 computer if they leave it in a hotel room. If you must leave your laptop computer unguarded, secure it by locking the machine to a heavy piece of furniture or arming it with a motion detector alarm.

4 Travel options promote well-being.

Carry spare car keys and house keys in a separate piece of luggage. Do not put your home address on luggage tags. Hometown luggage handlers won't be as tempted to visit your house while you are away. Learn how to run presentations from your personal digital assistant in the event that your computer is stolen.

5 Have five ways to get your money.

Consider carrying Automatic Teller Machine cards, credit cards, debit cards, checks and travelers checks. Carry a list of your credit cards with the toll-free numbers for canceling and replacing those cards. Keep a photo copy of your driver's license and/or passport in your luggage. Know how to obtain an emergency advance on your credit card and be familiar with wire services, foreign embassies and chambers of commerce in the areas that you visit.

5 Cool Ideas™
for Improved Public Speaking

There are many different types of public speaking, including seminars, training sessions and keynotes. I've developed 5 Cool Ideas for improved public speaking that will improve your game no matter what kind of speaking you do.

1   Meet the folks prior to talking with the folks.

This is an excellent way to build rapport and help the audience warm to you. You can greet people as they enter the room. If it's a small group, you may wish to personally visit them at their seats. Shake hands and thank audience members for attending. Ask what they hope to learn from the program. This psychological rhythm will help you become a much more effective speaker.

2   Smile at the beginning of your presentation.

Nervousness and anxiety will tug at your emotions, especially at the beginning of your speech. Remember to smile more than you normally would. In my early days of speaking, I would practice the beginning of my speech in a mirror. I would repeatedly greet my imaginary audience, each time giving the big smile I still use today. Be sure to let your voice smile, too. Use inflection and tone to demonstrate happiness and appreciation.

---

3 Never tell people that you're nervous.

Let the audience figure out if you're nervous. You've got limited time to convey your important message. Don't waste time saying the obvious. I once attended a training session given by a fellow speaker. Prior to the talk, he intimated to me that he had stopped wearing neckties in favor of sweaters. During the first few minutes of his talk, he found it necessary to tell the audience that he was wearing a sweater instead of tie. He damaged his credibility by stating the obvious. Also, avoid telling the audience that you're new to public speaking and that you're not a skilled orator. These comments can devalue your opinion and downgrade your authority. Hide your nervousness by minimizing your movement, especially early in the speech. Keep your hands out of your pockets.

4 Handouts can help deliver your message.

Give audience members a handout that explains how they can contact you. The handout can be a simple document highlighting your message. Your contact information will help people find you for future speeches.

5 Stand at the exit door to say "thank you."

At the end of the meeting, make a beeline for the exit door so you can say "good-bye" to audience members. This is a great way to personally thank people for attending your speech. On their way out, attendees will provide feedback, including compliments that will boost your confidence the next time you speak. Be sure to have business cards and a pen with you so that you don't need to leave your post when providing an autograph or your phone number.

5 Cool Ideas™
for Better Listening

Listening is a fantastic skill to develop because it can pay such big dividends. Listening skills can reduce stress, improve relationships, help you remember names and save time. Here are 5 Cool Ideas for better listening.

1 Good listeners practice listening.

Use your new skills to impress friends, business associates and yourself. I once earned a speaking engagement from "The Nation," the preeminent newspaper of Barbados by remembering the name of Executive Editor Roxanne Gibbs 20 minutes after meeting her and 30 other people. Roxanne was impressed and so was I. For *5 Cool Ideas for Remembering Names*, see page 66.

2 Use simple life moments to listen better.

Stop singing in the shower once in a while and listen. Listen to how the water sounds as it falls around you. Try to identify seven or eight different types of sounds. This simple exercise will teach you to hear nuances in group dynamics and in telephone conversations.

3 Listen to the bass line instead of the lyric.

When in the car, listen to songs you don't normally listen to. Listen to the musical arrangement instead of the lyrics. Try to identify the different instruments in the arrangement. Try listening to just one of the instruments, like the bass guitar.

---

4   Turn down the noise and tune in to life.

When you really start to pay attention to sound, you'll become aware of all the noise in our world. Block out some of the noise by wearing ear protection when flying, using vacuum cleaners and operating snowblowers. Listen to the important things and tune out extraneous offerings, like chatter. I remember being on a hike in the African bush. There was no traffic. There were no airplanes overhead and there was no electricity buzzing from nearby wires. All we could hear were birds chirping, the rustle of small rodents and a fellow hiker who would not shut his mouth.

5   Visual listening promotes connectivity.

Visual listening is a way to show regard for the speaker. By smiling and nodding your head, you relay encouragement to the speaker and promote connectivity. Leaning slightly forward and taking notes when people talk to you are also good listening habits. Don't hesitate to ask people to repeat themselves. Ask immediately so you don't feel embarrassed by asking later on.

5 Cool Ideas™
for Improving
Female Body Language

Many important signals are traded through non-verbal communication and what behavioral psychologists call Neuro-Linguistic Programming (NLP). Since women tend to be more emotive than men, ladies should be careful not to undermine their own communication by sending mixed signals. Inappropriate and incongruous signals rob women of their personal power. Here are 5 Cool Ideas for women to improve their body language.

1 Crossing your arms is not advisable.

According to behavioral psychologists, a woman who crosses her arms when she walks could be sending a signal that she is unapproachable or insecure. Of course, it could also mean that she's cold. Once, during one of my seminars, an older woman blamed the cover-up on men. "We cross our arms because men are always looking at our breasts," she huffed. Then she added, "And I cross my arms a lot lower than I used to."

2 Establish integrity with nonverbal cues.

Here are some easy ways for women to establish integrity. First, walk a little faster. This sends a signal that you have visible purpose. Your purposeful stride will generate a higher level of respect from others. Another idea is to avoid being too agreeable. During conversation, women have a tendency to nod their heads frequently, even if they don't agree with the speaker. Also, women have a tendency to slightly raise the pitch of their voice at the end of a sentence. What they say may come out as a question when it's meant to be a statement. Worse still, these unfortunate inflections may be interpreted as a persistant bid for approval.

3   Minimize major body movements, ladies.

Studies show that women make about four times more major movements per hour than men when seated in a boardroom setting. The movements include playing with jewelry, fussing with clothing, crossing and uncrossing legs and playing with hair.

4   Keep your hands away from your face.

Behavioral psychologists say that when a woman brushes her hair behind her ear, it is often interpreted as a "look at me" gesture. A sawing motion to scratch underneath her nose could mean that the woman is uncomfortable with something that is being said or done. Hands that linger near the neck can indicate preening. In a business setting, it's best to cut back on these signals rather than risk misinterpretation.

5   Act special to be perceived as special.

Use powerful women for role models. Observe Condoleeza Rice in the political arena. Check out Meg Whitman and Carli Fiorina from the business sector. All are positive role models for women.

5 Cool Ideas™
for Improving
Male Body Language

Neuro-Linguistic Programming (NLP) is another name for body language, the nonverbal cues we send with our eyes, hands and other body parts. Inappropriate or incongruous NLP robs men of their personal power. Here are 5 Cool Ideas for men to improve their body language.

1 Sustained eye contact will serve you well.

Most men are terrible with eye contact. Watch two men shake hands. One of them will invariably look away. Practice sustained eye contact by maintaining a visual connection for two or three seconds longer than you normally do. It'll take about 21 days to get used to this and then you'll enjoy it.

2 Take your hands out of your pockets.

Behavioral psychologists say that men who walk and talk with their hands in their pockets are sometimes conveying anxiety and insecurity. Why are we so uncomfortable with having our hands at the bottom of our arms? Take your hands out of your pockets and project personal power.

3 Smiling makes you more human.

According to brain dominance theory, discovered by Walter Sperry in the 1970s, men tend to be left-brain dominant. This means that they are rationally based,

---

rather than emotionally based. As a group, the male gender is not overly generous with facial expressions, which can make them difficult to read. When a man smiles frequently, he conveys confidence and competence. Be that man.

4   Open questions establish empathy.

Men can attract their greatest resource – other people – by using specific NLP techniques like forward listening and open questions. Forward listening is achieved by standing with one foot slightly in front of the other while slightly tilting the head. Closed questions like "How was your weekend?" generate brief responses. Open questions like, "What was your favorite part of the weekend?" initiate detailed conversations.

5   When you take note, others take note of you.

Men would be wise to use body language to reinforce their verbal messages. For example, if you want to send a signal that you are really paying attention to what someone is saying, take notes. In my booklet, *Hmmm... Little Ideas With Big Results*, I pose the question, "Do you believe what people do or what they say?" Actions, of course, speak louder than words. The *Hmmm...* booklet is available at www.EdisonHouse.com.

5 Cool Ideas™
for Building Better Relationships

When we build good relationships, we psychologically help others move closer to us. There are 15 words that will help get the job done. Presented as 5 Cool Ideas for building better relationships, here are the five most important words, the four most important words, the three most important words...

1   People want to hear "I am proud of you."

The five most important words you can use to build a relationship are, "I am proud of you." If you do not use these words every day, you are not telling people what they need to hear. "I am proud of you" is an emotion-based sentiment, which may be challenging for men to articulate. I had to practice saying this phrase before it was comfortable for me. As the eldest sibling in my family, I often practice on my brothers. One day, I called my brother Rob in New Orleans. "How are you?" I asked. "Good," he answered. "We finally closed on the house, the kids are in school and Kim's still talking to me." I said, "I'm impressed, Rob. You've moved the family twice in four years and kept all the wheels on the wagon. I'm proud of you." There was a slight pause as Rob wondered whether this was a prank call. "Thanks," he eventually said, psychologically taking a step toward me.

2 "What is your opinion?" shows you care.

The four most important words a person can use are "What is your opinion?" If you don't ask people for their opinion, they could think you don't care. Good communicators converse as if they are playing tennis. They hit the ball and then wait for someone to return it. Don't follow the ball over the net. Ask for opinions and listen.

3 "Would you please..." is still good etiquette.

The three most important words to build better relationships are "Would you please...?"

4 Saying "thank you" says a lot.

The simplest way to acknowledge appreciation and honor another person is to look him or her in the eye and say "thank you."

5 My name is my favorite word.

The most important word to use with another person is his or her name. You can maximize the power of persuasion by using the person's name in an imbedded phrase. "Try to do this in the future, okay Bob?" In the previous sentence, "okay Bob?" is an imbedded phrase.

5 Cool Ideas™
for Remembering Names

I once earned a speaking engagement by impressing Roxanne Gibbs, editor of "The Nation," a prominent Barbados newspaper. When I visited her company to deliver the presentation, Roxanne introduced me to a large group of her employees. She told them that I remembered her name a half-hour after meeting her and 30 other people in a buffet line. Here are 5 Cool Ideas for remembering names. It's how I got the gig.

1 Mnemonic triggers don't always work.

People who remember Pat's name because she is wearing purple, may struggle to recall her name when she wears brown. Try to remember a person by who they are, rather than what they wear.

2 Use "cluster imprinting" to learn names.

The goal of cluster imprinting is to imprint your brain with the person's name eight to ten times within three minutes of meeting them. Listen to the person say their name, then say "Catherine, it's nice to meet you." You've now heard her name twice.

3 Repetition is a form of practice.

After being introduced, you might say "Catherine, is that Catherine with a 'C' or Katherine with a 'K'?" The person could answer " 'Catherine' with a 'C'." Now you've heard the name six times and visualized it at least once. If someone approaches you and

---

Catherine, offer to introduce the new person. "Catherine, do you know David? David, this is Catherine." At this point, you've been imprinted with Catherine's name eight times.

4 Closing remarks are a chance to practice.

When it's time to excuse yourself, you might say "It's been nice meeting you, Catherine," which makes the ninth time your brain has been imprinted with her name. You are not likely to forget "Catherine."

5 Interval training can help achieve total recall.

Try to recall the name at several intervals during the next 24 hours, stretching the time span for each attempt. Another form of interval training is to review rosters and registration lists before and after the meeting.

5 Cool Ideas™
for Being a Better Joke Teller

My father had a terrific sense of humor. He only told good jokes and he could remember them forever. Below are 5 Cool Ideas for being a better joke teller and five jokes that illustrate each idea. These jokes have been published in my audio book, **Dear** Michael Angelo – A Father's Life Letters to His Son, *available at www.EdisonHouse.com.*

1 True stories can be funnier than fiction.
Musician Fritz Kreisler was invited by a haughty society matron to play violin at her upcoming house party. He set a fee of $1,000. The grand dame agreed but told him, "You will not mingle with my guests." "In that case," Kreisler said, "my fee will only be $500."

2 All humor pokes fun and critics are pokable.
A Viennese music critic died without leaving enough money for his burial. The critic's friends approached a well-known composer and asked him to contribute. "What's my share?" he asked. "Thirty kronen," they replied. The composer thought for a second and said, "Here's sixty kronen. Bury two critics."

3 Clever jokes are better than dirty jokes.
A wealthy matron was so proud of a valuable antique vase that she decided to have her bedroom painted the same color as the vase. Dozens of painters tried to match the shade, but none came close enough to satisfy the eccentric woman. Eventually, she located

a painter who successfully matched the color. The high society woman was very pleased with the results and made sure the entire art community learned the artist's name.

At an art show a few months later, several artists cornered the painter and asked him, "How did you get the walls to match that vase so perfectly?"

"I repainted the vase," the painter said.

4 Self-deprecating humor is a sure bet.

I bought a new necktie. I really liked the design and the colors but I had to take it back. The clerk asked me what was wrong with it and I told him. "It's too tight!"

5 Tell jokes using a series of three.

Three men were being considered for release from a mental institution. The release board asked the first candidate, "What's three times three?"

"One hundred and eighteen," he replied. The board chairman said, "Next!"

They asked the next patient the same question. "What's three times three?"

The second man said, "Tuesday." "Sorry, you're not ready yet, either. Next!"

They asked the third guy, "What's three times three?" The man said, "Nine."

"That's wonderful!" the interviewers exclaimed. "How did you arrive at the answer?"

"Easy," the man said, "I subtracted 118 from Tuesday."

5 Cool Ideas™
for Receiving Customer Satisfaction

Receiving excellent customer service should be effortless, but it is not. Getting satisfied can involve patience, impatience, negotiation and tactical strategy. Here are 5 Cool Ideas for achieving customer satisfaction.

1 Set yourself up for success.

The idea is to send signals to customer service representatives that you are to be taken seriously. It's always better to show them you're important rather than to tell them. The sentence "I spend a lot of money in your store" is not original and will probably not get you any extra attention. The clothes you wear are important so dress for success. Eye contact is important so remove your sunglasses.

2 Patience pays off.

Receiving good customer service should be easy. But sometimes you have to negotiate your satisfaction, almost coaxing it from reluctant service reps. You may need to make the same request of different people. When practical, start at the top and work down. If you must deal with a low-level clerk, always be polite, but firm. Always greet the person by saying "hello" and identifying yourself with your full name. Speak authoritatively without being brusque. If you receive a series of unsatisfactory answers, calmly state that "this is unacceptable" and begin using your tactical strategy. If you are speaking to a customer service representative on the telephone, know that you could be contacting them at a large call center, where reps of various proficiency answer the telephone. Don't hesitate to excuse yourself from the unhelpful person. Call back and you will likely reach another person who can be of more assistance.

3 Impatience pays off.

Use direct lines like, "Are you empowered to credit me for this inappropriate service charge?" and "This is my third request." Escalate, but don't get crazy.

4 Emotion cripples rational discussion.

Stay calm. In most cases, subtle techniques work better than histrionics. In a curious, non-confrontational tone, ask "What's your name?" Ask the service person how to spell it. Ask them their boss's name and how to spell that name. Your goal is to have the person recognize the intrinsic reward of honoring your request immediately. Utilize a strategy that clearly communicates the consequences of delayed customer service.

5 Use reward/consequence strategies.

Offer reward with comments like "You'll be a hero if you deal with this now" and "Let's take care of this today and no one else will have to get involved." Hint at consequence by saying things like "Can you help me with this or is it better to get your boss involved?" Keep excellent notes on the lack of customer service and you'll establish yourself as professional and credible. Record names, dates and the details. Spelling counts, especially with regard to names. See page 138 for *5 Cool Ideas for Creating Reward/Consequence Proposals*.

5 Cool Ideas™
for Being In Control

Everything we do has rewards and consequences. You can control various forms of this pleasure and pain depending on how well you understand the linkage between thoughts, emotions, behavior and reward. Thoughts, for example, usually lead to emotions. Emotions drive behavior. Behavior determines reward. Do you have complete control over your own thoughts, emotions and behavior? Here are 5 Cool Ideas for being in control.

1   Own your own stuff and be in control.

Miguel Ruiz writes in his book *The Four Agreements* that we need to control our own thoughts and emotions. When we own our own stuff, we can limit others' control of our stuff.

2   You should own your thoughts, I think.

Controlling your own thoughts is based on the concept of free will, which means that you are responsible and accountable for your own thinking. Not to put thoughts in your head, but this seems like a "no-brainer," doesn't it? If, for example, you study the odds of winning the lottery and decide that you have a very slim chance of winning, you will probably decide not to play.

3   Own your emotions, including sadness.

Thoughts help determine emotions. If you decide not to play the lottery, you will probably not feel like buying a ticket. Being in control of your emotions doesn't mean that you cannot cry. At my mother's funeral service, I wept like a child. I wept like a child *and I was in complete control of my emotions.* I was in control because it was totally appropriate to cry when my mother died. I think that if your mother dies and you don't cry, you may not have control of your emotions.

4 Be 100% responsible for your behavior.

Emotions drive behavior. In our lottery example, if you don't feel like purchasing a ticket, you will not win the lottery. Of course, no one can ever make you buy a lottery ticket. No one can ever make you do anything you don't want to do, if you own your behavior. In almost every situation, a person has options. If a wife insists that her husband quits bowling because Tuesday night is scouting night for their son, the husband has at least two options. The husband could quit bowling and then hold his wife in contempt because she made him quit. Another option is for the husband to quit bowling and be happy with the behavior that allows him to spend more time with his son.

5 Owning your stuff is owning your reward.

Many people do not profess to have control over their own reward and consequence because it is easier to blame others for our failure. When we take ownership of our own life equation – that thoughts lead to emotions, emotions drive behavior and behavior determines reward – we will stop blaming others for our lack of success.

5 Cool Ideas™
for Dealing With Difficult People

Difficult people are everywhere. We meet them at work, in the service industry and even at home. Difficult personalities will ruin your day if you let them. Handle difficult people using Personal Power and the "You Can't Hurt Me" technique. Here are 5 Cool Ideas for dealing with difficult people.

1 Everyone has Personal Power.

Predatory personalities will sometimes use their power to negatively influence you. Bosses who micro-manage will try to leverage their Position Power. Large people may try to intimidate you with Physical Power. It's important for you to remember that you have a huge amount of Personal Power, which can trump all other types of power, if used strategically and responsibly.

2 Power is traded through signals.

Neuro-linguistic programming (NLP) refers to the patterned behavior commonly known as "body language." Think of NLP as an exchange of nonverbal signals. Hands and eyes, for example, can be terrific indicators of what someone is really thinking. NLP experts have discovered that liars and other difficult people tend to look up and to their right when they are uncomfortable with what they are saying. Send me an e-mail if you would like to receive a chart of eye signals and what they mean. Ask for the "NLP Cues," in the subject line. My e-mail address is MichaelCaruso@EdisonHouse.com.

---

3   We should help weak links become strong.

In his book, *The 21 Irrefutable Laws of Leadership*, John Maxwell reminds us that a person known as a "weak link" deserves to be a "strong link" on another chain. Use reward/consequence proposals to encourage the person to transfer to that other chain. See page 138 for *5 Cool Ideas for Creating Reward/Consequence Proposals*.

4   You can't change other people.

You can't control others, but you can control your reaction to them. When dealing with angry people, for example, enjoy the results of responding rather than reacting. A reaction is an immediate, emotional form of communication that compromises your effectiveness with difficult people. A response, on the other hand, is a time-delayed, cerebral form of communication. Delaying your response by two or three seconds can make you more effective with problem personalities.

5   You can't hurt me.

The concept of "You Can't Hurt Me" was first published in my *Hmmm…* booklet, which is available at www.EdisonHouse.com. The concept states that people cannot emotionally harm you unless you allow them to. People who use "You Can't Hurt Me," send signals that convey Personal Power. They convey these signals when they are shaking hands (using sustained eye contact, a firm grip and a pleasant expression), entering a room (with a confident smile and purposeful stride) and speaking (using an excellent vocabulary, good diction and timely pauses).

5 Cool Ideas™
for Diffusing an Angry Person

Hostile people can really push buttons. They rant against guilty and sometimes innocent parties. Angry at some real or perceived injustice, irate individuals burn every bridge in their path. Here are 5 Cool Ideas for diffusing an angry person.

1 Interrupt the rant under two conditions.

Angry people can teach us things about our business, our products, our services and ourselves. Learning from angry people can be challenging because the moment is infused with discomfort and drama. Listen to the rant for a few minutes to see what you can learn from the disgruntled person. Interrupt the rant when the person becomes repetitive or abusive.

2 Use loud, neutral noise to stay focused.

You must interrupt to help the angry person recapture his or her emotions. The interruption must be loud enough to match the person's volume and intensity. Neutral noise is less likely to aggravate the bull. Try clapping your hands or shouting the person's name.

3 Charging the bull is not a safe strategy.

Aggressive people are good at emotionally charging you. They take no prisoners and gear up for the drama. Don't play their game. Yell the bull's name to interrupt with loud, neutral noise. Then, lower your volume to a whisper tone as you add, "Let's sit down

---

and work this out. I think I have a solution you'll like." Admonish your children in a whisper tone and kids will look at each other and say, "Mom's really mad this time. She didn't even yell."

4 Emotion cripples rational discussion.

When you interrupt the rant to sustitute your yelling, it's like throwing gasoline on the fire. There's nothing gained when your blood pressure goes up and steam comes out of your ears. In fact, losing your temper is one way the angry person knows he's getting to you. Stay calm and remain in control. Silently count to five before responding. Waiting gives you extra time to think and will drive angry people crazy.

5 Reframe the conversation in civility.

There are several ways to bring the angry person back to planet earth. Whatever method you use, remember that you're in control. After all, the angry person usually wants something from you. Try to get angry people to sit down so they calm down. Announce a five-minute break without asking their permission. They are likely to be calmer when you return. If they are not calmer when you return, announce another five-minute break. If speaking to an angry person on the telephone, excuse yourself for 60 seconds so you can "take care of something." Press the hold button and breath. Return to the call and calmly say, "Thank you. I really needed to take care of that. Now, how can I help you?" Psychologists tell us that anger is rooted in fear. Address the fear and anger will subside.

5 Cool Ideas™
for Solving Problems

Once upon a time, a truck got stuck driving under an overpass. City engineers, trucking company owners and law enforcement officials argued about how to drive the truck out from under the bridge without causing more damage to the vehicle or the overpass. Traffic backed up and tempers flared as the experts debated possible solutions. They considered taking the wheels off the truck and even shearing off the top of the truck to provide the necessary clearance. One radical plan involved lifting the bridge to allow the truck to be driven out. Finally a 7-year-old boy tugged on a policeman's sleeve and asked, "Why don't you just let the air out of the tires and drive the truck out?" Here are 5 Cool Ideas for solving problems.

1 Enlist your right-brain to solve problems.

Most people use the left side of the brain when solving problems. According to brain dominance theory, discovered by Walter Sperry in the early 1970s, the left hemisphere of the brain specializes in linear thinking. The right side of the brain encourages creativity and innovation. Use your right brain to increase efficiency when solving problems. As a bonus, you'll have more fun.

2 Multiple ideas generate innovative solutions.

Let's say you want to go from one place to another. You can almost always choose between several modes of transportation and routes. All of the various choices solve the problem of getting you from point A to point B. There are always several ways to solve a problem. Be open to multiple ideas and enjoy innovative solutions.

3 Get outside, next to and underneath the box.

The problem as stated is rarely the true problem. Restate the problem five ways. Change the wording. Take different viewpoints. If you can't make it better, make it worse and see what happens.

4 Search for multiple solutions.

The first solution found is usually inadequate or non-optimum. Suspend judgement and criticism when first collecting ideas. Be crazy and try all your ideas. Try other people's ideas. In school, we are taught to find the correct answer and move on. When problem solving, it is important to ask the correct *questions*. Keep asking "What else might work?"

5 Strive for "planned serendipity."

Nobel Laureate physicist, Richard Feynman, believed in getting his hands dirty and doing lots of experiments. He said, "To develop working ideas efficiently, I tried to fail as fast as I could."

5 Cool Ideas™
for Dealing With Procrastination

People put things off for hundreds of reasons, but most of their excuses can be traced to five core issues: lack of urgency, disorganization, hero syndrome, ego and the fact that the procrastinator is enabled. Here are 5 Cool Ideas for dealing with procrastination.

1 Urgency can eliminate procrastination.

Automobile accidents and serious illnesses almost always create a sense of urgency. Try to get the procrastinator to appreciate urgency without making a trip to the hospital.

2 Folks who are organized don't procrastinate.

When we are disorganized, it's harder to be focused. A messy work space, an overly busy schedule and consistent tardiness indicate disorganization. By insisting on organization for 21 days, the offender has the opportunity to develop a new habit. Behavioral psychologists suggest it takes most people three weeks to make or break a habit.

3 Ego can make someone chronically late.

Some procrastinators want to send a message that their time is more important than your time. I used to have a problem with being on time. Once, when I arrived late to a movie theatre, my brother Joe asked me, "Is your time more important than my time?" This simple question underscored my ego problem and I tried to never keep him waiting again.

---

4   Give procrastinators a "hero's welcome."

A person with "Hero Syndrome" needs to feel important. Walking into a meeting late or delivering a project one-minute before deadline somehow provides necessary drama for the procrastinator. If the procrastinator insists on a Hero's Entrance, you might try giving him a Hero's Welcome. Use positive or negative forms of attention to influence behavior. If this doesn't work, you might tell him that his tardiness has caused him to forfeit your time together. Another technique is to lock the door when the meeting begins, denying the procrastinator entrance.

5   Enablers help procrastinators to be late.

By not confronting a procrastinator, you are actually enabling them. On the final day of a two-day seminar I was teaching, a woman apologized for being tardy on both days. She said, "I'm always five minutes late. I lose all track of time." I said "Which is it, you're always late or you lose all track of time?" When I didn't accept her behavior or her explanation I disqualified myself as an enabler. This encouraged the woman to identify the real reason for her tardiness. The woman admitted that she typically leaves five minutes late, which was the real issue in the first place.

5 Cool Ideas™
for Managing Time

Time is a resource shared by everyone from Nobel Prize winners to paupers. Hyrum Smith, founder of the Franklin Planner time management system, tells of a man who approached him to say, "I wish I lived 100 years ago when they had more time." Everyone has the same amount of time. It's how we manage time that makes a difference. People who manage their time always have enough time. Here are 5 Cool Ideas on how to better manage your time.

1 The first hour of the day sets the tone.

Be very selfish with your first 60 minutes of consciousness. I have a "Power Hour" that helps me wake up individual body parts, provides consistent exercise and allows daily professional development. See page 136 for *5 Cool Ideas for Your Power Hour.*

2 Do the most important task first.

Be selfish with the first 60 minutes of your work day, too. Most people spend the first hour of the work day greeting coworkers, getting coffee, browsing e-mail, sifting through junk mail and generally anticipating the day. Professional development guru Dr. Stephen Covey writes in *The Seven Habits of Highly Effective People* that we should do the most important task of the day first. It follows that if we get only one thing done that day, we have spent our time wisely.

---

3   Use resources to prevent wasted time.

Waiting rooms and traffic jams are terrific opportunities to sneak in a couple pages of professional development. Traffic congestion became much less frustrating when I realized that it was an opportunity to do more reading, er, listening. That's why I always have an audiobook in my car. If you keep a book handy, you aren't wasting time in the doctor's waiting room, you're learning something new.

4   "Pre-call" your allotted time.

Your day consists of chunks of time. When you manage those chunks of time, you'll have a better day. Maximize time, for example, by limiting casual conversation. Begin such conversations by "pre-calling" the amount of time you have available. If you tell someone you only have five minutes to chat, they are more likely to honor your time frame. Be sure to excuse yourself after five minutes. After all, if you don't honor your time, why should others?

5   Book appointments with yourself.

Block out chunks of time for yourself by literally booking appointments with the most important person in the world – you.

5 Cool Ideas™
for Saving Money

Rocker David Lee Roth once said, "Money can't buy happiness, but it will buy you a big enough yacht to sail right up next to it." Here are 5 Cool Ideas for saving enough money to buy that yacht.

1   There are two basic ways to save money.

The first way to save money is to generate more revenue. The second way to save money is to reduce expenses. Many people struggle with these basic concepts. Credit cards can complicate spending habits because time-delayed expenses usually translate into high interest rates. Paying the balance within 30 days would eliminate interest payments, but according to the folks at Motley Fool, 1.3 million credit card holders declare bankruptcy every year. Reduce credit card debt by paying at least twice the minimum balance every month until the debt is reduced to zero. Carry only two low-interest credit cards, one exclusively for emergencies. Pay off your credit cards every month.

2   Spending is emotional and habit forming.

Point of purchase displays thrive on impulse buyers. This type of "I must have it now" behavior is a sure sign that you are engaged in emotional spending, a practice that is costing you money in more ways than one. A $2 latté on the way to work equals $500 a year (250 work days times $2). Buy a $2 latté every day for five years and you'll spend $2,500 on steamed milk. Money spent on lattés is spent through habit rather than planning.

3 **Planning expenditures will save you money.**
Planned spending provides a kind of satisfaction that
impulse buying does not. When you work within a
budget and strategize your buying process, you will
feel more deserving of the product or service. Plan
four major purchases you want to make in the next
two years. Estimate how much they will cost and
work them into your budget. Do not spend more than
$100 for anything that is not in your plan.

4 **When you track your money, you control it.**
Track your expenditures weekly, monthly and yearly.
Hold a weekly meeting with your significant other to
discuss progress and to celebrate small victories. You
do not need to buy anything to celebrate.

5 **Time can work for you or against you.**
According to *Money Management*, by Peter Jeppson
and Alan Williams, an average person earns about
$1,600,000 in his or her lifetime. That same average
person usually saves only 3% of their life earnings
and will thus possess a mere $57,000 in total assets
at age 65. Be sure to save enough money for retirement. Project your ideal monthly retirement income,
then determine how much more money you'll need
to be comfortable. Stocks, bonds and mutual funds
can help get you there, but good old compound interest is the goose that always lays the golden egg.

5 Cool Ideas™
for Being More Persuasive

During a trip to Egypt, I had the opportunity to ride a camel. My encounter with the camel's keeper inspired me to create 5 Cool Ideas for increasing your powers of persuasion.

1 Positive expectation invites persuasion.

I've done a lot of cool things in my life. I've played rock music in a country bar, I've snorkeled in the waters of Maui and I've taken exciting baths with my brothers, although not recently. Nothing, however, has matched the thrill of riding a camel. My positive anticipation was not lost on the camel steward. He knew from my expression that I had always dreamed of riding a camel next to the pyramids. Once aboard the camel, my guide led the beast a few steps before looking up at me to ask, "Are you happy?" My answer to this question was a resounding "Yes!" confirming my positive expectations for the steward and essentially inviting him to be persuasive.

2 To be assertive is to be persuasive.

The camel steward's objective was to receive a good size tip. He was correct in assuming that if I was happy with his services, I would reward him with some extra money. When I admitted that I was happy, he held out his hand and said, "Now would be a good time to show me your appreciation."

---

3 Persistence offers its own rewards.

I gave the camel steward some Egyptian pounds. He smiled and immediately asked for more. Surprised with his bravado, yet delighted with his services, I surprised myself by giving him more money. His persistence had paid off for him. To paraphrase Calvin Coolidge, "Neither talent, genius nor education can take the place of persistence. Persistence and determination are omnipotent."

4 Persuasion should allow everyone to win.

The camel steward won because he received a healthy tip. I won because I received exceptional service. The steward provided props for photographs and arranged some special poses. He even made the camel smile! Arrange for everyone to win and persuasion will always feel good.

5 Persuasion should not be manipulative.

After the camel ride, my guide told me it was a pleasure doing business with me. Surprisingly, this minimized my buyer's remorse for possibly overtipping him. In the final analysis, he was persuasive without being offensive. Acknowledging persuasion helps minimize ill effects of the process and sets the stage for future persuasion.

5 Cool Ideas™
for Better Table Etiquette

Good etiquette sends powerful signals about who you are. A steady stream of dinner keynotes has helped me polish my table manners and I'm still learning. Etiquette expert Leslie Jacobs of Leslie Jacobs Associates, Inc. contributed to these 5 Cool Ideas for behaving yourself at the dinner table.

1 The napkin is your friend.

If a napkin is in your glass, wait for the server to offer it to you. Otherwise, place your napkin in your lap after everyone is seated and after the host has done so. Open the napkin as you move it to your lap. Fold it once into a triangle, placing the base of the triangle below your waist. Use the napkin to wipe your mouth before drinking. When excusing yourself, place the loosely bunched napkin on the seat of your chair. When you are finished eating, bunch the napkin and lay it to the left of your plate, but only after everyone is done with their meals.

2 Silverware sends signals.

Blame the Europeans for the plethora of utensils at formal place settings. Silverware protocol is easier than you might think. Eat from the outside in. The fork furthest to the left is for salad, while the innermost fork is reserved for the entree. When eating, keep silverware completely on the plate. If you're temporarily leaving the table or simply going on about yourself, lay down your utensils with the tips of your fork (always tines down) and knife crossed in the middle of the plate. The tines should face 2 o'clock and the knife (always with the edge towards you) should face 10 o'clock. When you're finished with a course, place the knife and fork on the rim of the plate, parallel to each other, both facing 10 o'clock.

3   Solids to the left, liquids to the right.

Which glass should I use? Which bread plate is mine? I'm so confused. Here's how it works. That's your bread plate on the left. The glasses near the knives are yours. Hold white wine glasses by the stem to allow the wine to remain chilled. Hold red wine goblets the same or if you know what you're doing, by the bottom of the glass. Ladies, use your napkin to pat your lipstick before your first sip, so you don't stain the glass. Gentlemen, don't drink with food in your mouth and don't make me tell you again.

4   Don't touch the flatware.

The wait staff doesn't need your help, okay? Let them do their job. You just sit there and look good. Speaking of looking good, never push your plate away when finished eating.

5   Attention to detail will get you invite back.

I have three more details for you to remember. First, gentlemen should rise when a lady returns to the table. If she doesn't return, it's because you didn't rise when she left the table. Second, food should leave your mouth the way it goes in. You eat an olive with a fork so remove the pit with a fork. There are two exceptions to this rule. If you eat a grape that has seeds, remove the seeds with a napkin, then discreetly return the seeds to your plate. If you eat fish that has bones, it's okay to use your fingers to remove the bones from your mouth. Lastly, dip the spoon away from you when eating soup. Use the furthest rim of the bowl to clear soup from under the utensil.

5 Cool Ideas™
for Men's Style

Clothes are signals and people judge you by the signals you send. When you wear clothes that have become lifeless and limp, people will likely think of you as lifeless and limp. Automatic washers and even dry cleaning procedures can eventually wring the life out of clothes. Most men would do well to donate three of their shirts to Goodwill, which might force them to upgrade their wardrobe. Here are 5 Cool Ideas for men's style.

1 Dress like you own the place.

A sport coat sends a signal that the person wearing it is going places. Wear a jacket when you walk into a room. You can always throw it over a chair, if you are overdressed. Always wear a sport coat or suit coat when you are holding a meeting or giving a presentation.

2 Button the jacket to hide the gut.

A single-button coat need only be buttoned when you're holding a meeting or giving a presentation. A double-breasted coat should always be buttoned. Put a pocket square or handkerchief into the breast pocket. Get one for all of your suits and sport coats so you don't have to play "Find the Pocket Square" when getting dressed.

3 Here's a better idea – lose the gut.

A big belly says so much about you. It says that you enjoy life and that you're a good eater. It says that your wife is a great cook and that you're a good provider. Your bulging abdomen could also convey that you're lazy and that you don't like exercise. A big belly often indicates a lack of discipline and self-respect.

4 A collared shirt shows class.

T-shirts and Henleys are fine around the yard, but if you're going out, show some class and wear a collared shirt. It sends a signal that you are upscale and well-groomed. I have found collars especially helpful in gaining quality customer service such as hotel room upgrades.

5 Polished shoes are a good reflection of you.

Shoes are a great indicator of their owner's character and attention to detail. Wipe off shoes after you come in from inclement weather. Keep a fresh coat of polish on them and send signals that you are on top of things. When you send signals that you are attentive to details, new team members don't have to wonder about you. Show difficult people that you have good character and they are less likely to bother you.

5 Cool Ideas™
for Creating Memories

Human beings are creatures of habit. We are more likely to do things we've done before than to try something new. We drive the same route to work every day, park in the same spot when we get there and eat the same types of lunches from week to week. This "routine-groove-rut" is exactly the kind of patterned behavior that prevents us from making new memories. Here are 5 Cool Ideas on how to create new memories.

1 Living in the past doesn't create memories.

People who dwell on the past often develop a victim mentality about life. Victims perceive life to be a series of negative occurrences because of things that have happened *to* them. Their attitude might be "People have always taken advantage of me, therefore, I am not interested in meeting new people." Old scripts can be keeping you from enjoying new material.

2 Invite new memories by rewriting your slate.

Imprinting is a series of repetitive life lessons that help us determine our view of the world, including our self-concept. Most of us are indelibly imprinted early in life. Philosopher John Locke wrote that, as youngsters, our minds are "tabula rasa" or a blank slate. Early on, people write on our slates, helping us create memories. Some of us have trouble writing over those old memories. When you can rewrite your slate, you can easily add new memories. Computer experts might describe rewriting your slate as overwriting your disk.

---

3 Accept that new invitation.

A female friend of mine was jogging when she encountered a group of strange men. The men identified themselves as secret service agents traveling with then President George Herbert Walker Bush. My friend told me that the agents invited her to run with the President and his entourage the next morning. She passed on the offer. I asked her why she declined such a unique opportunity and my friend said, "I guess I didn't feel like it." Doing new things avails us to new memories, so make it a habit to step out of your routine. Memories are generated by a process behavioral psychologists refer to as "experiential learning." New experiences, of course, are a form of imprinting, which helps us to create memories. Routines do not promote newness.

4 The present is sometimes too predictable.

People who only think about the present condition are so caught up in routines that they cannot seem to try new things. In their determined effort to maintain status quo, they resist new opportunities, thus stifling the creation of new memories.

5 Live as if you don't have much time left.

Sociologists have discovered that people near death have one overwhelmingly common regret about their life. They usually regret not trying more new things like travelling to foreign countries and meeting more people. What have you always wanted to do? What would you do this year if you knew it would be your last year? Use the answers to these questions as incentive to generate new memories.

5 Cool Ideas™
for Building a Legacy

A legacy is a "leave-behind" for future workers and family members. Legacy can be created at work, at home and through personal service. Here are 5 Cool Ideas for building legacy.

1   People who appreciate legacy will leave one.

Develop an appreciation for legacy. Creating a powerful and influential leave-behind can be inexpensive and easy, especially if created a little at a time. To learn more about what constitutes legacy and how you can create legacy using your thoughts and words, read Mitch Albom's terrific book, *Tuesdays With Morrie* and listen to my audiobook, *Dear Michael Angelo – A Father's Life Letters to His Son*, available at www.EdisonHouse.com.

2   Your "leave-behind" can be simple.

Building legacy does not have to consume large amounts of time. Many people leave a legacy by documenting their own life. You can document your life by writing a series of letters, recording stories on audiotape and videotape, building a website and keeping a journal. Establish internal deadlines to help keep you on track. To write a 12-chapter book on your life, finish one chapter every month and you'll be finished in a year.

3 Journals are an accumulative form of legacy.

Write down your important thoughts and experiences in a journal. Spend time developing themes like "self-esteem" and "happiness" rather than capturing "Dear Diary" ramblings. Give extra attention to stories that teach a life lesson. You might choose to create computer documents for each important concept. Store them in a "Legacy" file on your home computer. Make sure to backup your data.

4 Your correspondence is your diary.

You're probably creating legacy with the e-mails that you generate and receive every day. The easiest way to document this activity is to send yourself a copy of the compelling messages that you compose. Save e-mails to a "Legacy" file. After a few years, review your collection and you'll begin to notice trends in your correspondence that might offer clarity and congruity to the story of your life.

5 Ask your Mom or Dad to write you a letter.

Ask your parents to create a theme letter by writing what success means to them or by sending a list of their five happiest moments. If Mom or Dad only write one letter, it will be a masterpiece. If your parents have passed on, it's time for you to write some letters to your children. Write time-delayed letters. Mail the letter to your own home. When it arrives, write on the envelope, "For Johnny to open on his 16th birthday" or "For Jane to open on her wedding day." I have written letters to my unborn children, which will hopefully help them develop an appreciation for legacy.

5 Cool Ideas™
for a Good Life

Sometime ago, I developed a formula for a good life. If you read good books and see good movies, eat good food and drink good wine, have good friends and think good thoughts – you will have a good life. Here are 5 Cool Ideas for having that good life.

1   Read good books to establish "forced flow."

The New York Times Best Seller List is a great place to find quality titles. The list is published in the Sunday edition. From the list, I've enjoyed Miguel Ruiz's *The Four Agreements*, which taught me how to not harm myself with my own words. The New York Times also introduced me to Eric Schlosser's *Fast Food Nation – The Dark Side of the American Meal*, which taught me how to not harm myself with my own food. A constant flow of good information has undoubtedly contributed to my good life.

2   Films that win awards, offer rewards.

My favorite movies make me laugh, cry and think. Make good decisions when you plunk down $9 per ticket and more importantly, carefully consider how you spend a two-hour block of your time. Look for movies that have been nominated for Golden Globe awards or Oscars. Enjoy a balance between car crashes and subtitles.

---

3   Good food is fresh food.

Include at least one vegetable at breakfast. Don't eat potato chips at all. Find a way to measure the food you eat. Some people track calories or the weight of the food. I count fat grams and generally allow myself no more than 35 grams of fat per day. As a result, I feel good almost all the time.

4   Have good, safe friends.

Do you have "safe" friends that keep you insulated from negativity? Do your friends help you feel better about yourself? Do they teach you new things and challenge your thinking? If not, it may be time to make some new friends. Remember that in order to spend time with new friends, you probably need to spend less time with old friends. This is okay.

5   Think good thoughts and be rewarded.

Positive thinking is critical. Optimism sets the stage for the life equation, which states that thoughts help determine emotion, emotion drives behavior and behavior delivers rewards. See page 72 for *5 Cool Ideas for Being in Control*. Good thoughts put everything in motion. What do you think?

5 Cool Ideas™
for New Year's Resolutions

Anytime is a good time for resolutions. The most successful resolutions offer anticipation of reward or the avoidance of pain. Freud wrote that pleasure and pain are terrific motivators. Here are 5 Cool Ideas for New Year's resolutions.

1   Be purposeful in everything you do.

You can become much more efficient by striving for purpose in your daily activities. Do you just eat lunch or do you enrich relationships while you eat? What purpose do those two sitcoms serve you every night? What is the purpose of eating that bag of chips? More importantly, what types of consequences await you now that you've indulged? Be purposeful in everything you do. Walk with purpose and people will be more likely to respect your time.

2   Resolve not to be mediocre.

Use the freshness of the new year as an excuse for avoiding mediocrity. This can be a challenging task because industry markets products and services to the lowest common denominator. Junk food is marketed to the lowest common denominator. Fast food, for example, is produced cheaply and sold cheaply. Sitcom television is geared toward the masses. The people who produce sitcoms even provide a laugh track so that you'll know when most people laugh. Give yourself an upgrade. Resolve to distance yourself from the lowest common denominator.

---

3 Schedule your exercise.

Exercise is more effective when it is regular and systematic. It can be difficult to schedule exercise unless time is pre-committed. I've inserted 40 push-ups and 100 sit-ups into my Power Hour, my first 60 minutes of consciousness. See page 136 for *5 Cool Ideas for Your Power Hour.*

4 Mend fences and help others resolve issues.

The new year is the perfect time to mend a broken relationship. Call, or better yet, visit the person you want to make peace with. Use this exact wording: "I feel bad about what's happened between us and want to take responsibility for everything. I'm sorry about the past and I'm going to be a better person for you in the future." Whether the other party accepts your apology, rebuffs you or otherwise tries to continue the conversation, do not pursue the topic. Allow them to respond, then gracefully end the meeting or phone call. Give the person time to think about what you said. Monitor feedback and if things don't improve after you've apologized, consider replacing the relationship.

5 Service clubs are life-long resolutions.

Viktor Frankl, author of *Man's Search for Meaning*, wrote that life's meaning comes from serving a cause greater than oneself. Rotary, Optimist International and the Big Brother/Big Sister organizations have helped me achieve meaning in my life. These types of service clubs give back to the community while helping members feel better about themselves. If you want to feel better about yourself, do something for someone else. Happy New Year!

5 Cool Ideas™
for Motivation

I'm not a motivational speaker. I'm more...
aggravational. I pose questions that get underneath
people's skin. Attend my seminar and receive the
ominous warning: "Pain will find you." My tech-
nique is to propose scenarios that allow audience
members to choose between reward and negative
consequence. When confronted with making a choice
between pleasure or pain, people become motivated.
Here are 5 Cool Ideas for motivation.

1 There is always reward or consequence.

For everything we do, there is either reward or consequence. For everything we *don't* do, there is reward or consequence, as well. Reward and negative
consequence are terrific motivators. When we as-
sess a situation and make a good decision about what
to do, we proactively generate a desirable result. That
desired result reinforces our need to be rewarded
again.

2 You never get to win the management game.

You just get to keep playing. And you only get to
keep playing if you think five moves ahead of negative angels, underperformers and passive-aggressive
personalities. For that matter, you never get to win
the sales game or the relationship game either. My
friend and coach Joe Gilliam reminds me that the
only way to keep five moves ahead is to continually
process new information.

---

3   Cancel negative info with positive info.

Negative angels deliver demotivating messages like "you're not good enough" and "that idea would never work." Negative angels can be coworkers, angry customers, bosses and family members. Positive angels deliver motivating messages like "you're exceptional" and "you can do it." Positive angels can be coworkers, angry customers, bosses and of course, family members. Positive angels can also be authors, seminar leaders and dead people, like Martin Luther King and Benjamin Franklin.

4   Pain will find you.

How's that for a motivational and upbeat idea? Like it or not, life will have pain and discomfort. Jobs will go away, natural disasters will occur and people will die. The goal is to be prepared for such situations by establishing a network of quality friends, a cache of material resources and a good outlook to help get you through the tough times.

5   Priming the pump will keep you motivated.

In order to be motivated, you must take care of yourself. Get plenty of sleep and balance your schedule with work and play. Eliminate enough television time to allow for regular exercise and trips to the museum. Eat right because if you don't feel good about your life, you will never able to help others feel good about their lives.

5 Cool Ideas™
for Dealing with Negative People

Negative people are always recruiting. The trick to dealing with them is to understand their psychology and to counter them with positive angels. Here are 5 Cool Ideas for dealing with negative people.

1 **Use positive angels to quell negative angels.**
Negative people say things like "you're not good enough" and "you can't do that." They dwell on what you're lacking rather than what you offer. Counter the messages from negative angels with messages from positive angels, who say "you can do that."

2 **Negative people cannot be converted.**
Negative people use words that grammarians refer to as "absolutes." Absolutes are words like "always" and "never." These words help negative people validate their pessimistic viewpoint. They say "I always have to do this job" and "Tom never has to do this job." Listen for negative people to say "Nobody ever listens to me." To deal with the negative person, prove the exception to their statement. If the negative person says "I never win anything" you might ask "Didn't you win the big stuffed animal at the holiday party?" Having quickly proved the exception to their statement, you then wink and smile to keep things light. Softly say, "I see how you are" as you walk away. Rather than try to change the person, simply terminate the discussion. A positive person can never truly win over a negative person because negative people will not be converted.

---

3 Distance yourself.

Of course, you must walk away from negative people or risk being sucked into their world. Distance yourself from negative people whether you work with them or live with them. Negative people will bring you down. They have unlimited energy and amazing stamina.

4 Practice self-subjugation – go "Columbo."

Peter Falk played a bumbling police lieutenant named Columbo on television. Lt. Columbo seemed so inept, that by comparison, his nemesis felt intellectually superior. Columbo had a very effective technique for dealing with problematic people. The lieutenant would tap his temple and say "Help me understand." When your whiner says something like "Nobody ever listens to me," go "Columbo." Say "Help me understand. Wasn't that you and me in your office last Tuesday? We talked about this very issue. How can you say nobody ever listens to you? Does my time mean nothing to you?" Then wink and smile to keep things light. Say, "I see how you are" and walk away.

5 Fly with positive angels.

Learn to evaluate people according to their "safety factor." Unsafe people leave you feeling unconfident, disenchanted and out of sorts. Safe people help you feel good about yourself.

5 Cool Ideas™
for Bargain Hunting

It's not easy to get a good deal. There is a real science to bargain hunting that involves techniques like flinching and concession leveraging. Bargain hunting has a specific protocol. Never use your bargaining to financially take advantage of people. Always thank the other party for a good deal and avoid gloating no matter how good the bargain. Here are 5 Cool Ideas for bargain hunting.

1 As a customer, your value fluctuates.

As a potential customer, you may have less value when the salesperson is having a busy day or a good month. You may be worth more if he or she hasn't made quota or if the product is running out of shelf time. Get as much information as possible about your value as a customer.

2 Get the salesperson to spend time with you.

When the salesperson invests time and energy with you, they are more likely to offer you a concession. This is especially true if your salesperson is empowered to make a deal.

3 Flinching can be fun and profitable.

No matter what price is quoted, flinch as if hearing that price is the most painful sound you've ever heard. It is not possible to overly dramatize the flinch, so have fun with it. If your flinch is effective, the salesperson will immediately apologize for offending you and offer some sort of concession.

---

4   Use one concession to get another.

When the first concession is offered, remember to pause as if you are unimpressed. Then ask, "Is that the best you can do?" The amount of time you wait for the first concession is an indicator of how long you'll wait for the second offer. Also, the depth and value of the first concession indicates the likelihood of an even better deal. Leverage the second concession to get the third.

5   Know exactly what you want.

Determine which concessions are most important to you prior to the negotiation. You must be very sure about what concessions appeal to you because the salesperson is not likely to volunteer exactly what you want. If you want to pay no more than $200 for a refrigerator, commit to that price going into the negotiation. Concessions on a fridge could include a price break, a discounted floor model, a longer warranty, free delivery, no sales tax, more favorable payment terms and a discount if you purchase a matching stove at the same time. No matter how the deal turns out, be sure to thank the salesperson for being helpful. Compliment his or her negotiating skills. After all, you couldn't have gotten a good deal without the other person's help.

5 Cool Ideas™
for Sounding Intelligent

When our words are simple and repetitive, people will likely regard us as simple and repetitive. When our words have depth and nuance, people will usually perceive us as having depth and nuance. Here are 5 Cool Ideas for sounding more intelligent.

1 A strong vocabulary is always impressive.

Speech can become lazy and compromised if we don't remain diligent. For example, the phrase, "I could care less," is often substituted for the more appropriate phrase, "I couldn't care less." You will sound more intelligent when you subscribe to an e-mail service that sends you a new vocabulary word every day. Most of the on-line dictionaries do this. To practice my word-of-the-day, I call my brother Rob.

"How's it going, Rob?" I asked.

"Great," Rob said. "I went to a seminar on Monday and learned a lot."

"I'm glad you're going to seminars. That's lifelong learning, you know. That's how you become erudite."

Rob said, "That's the word-of-the-day, isn't it?"

"Yep."

"What's it mean?"

"Smart."

"Thanks for calling, Mike."

"You're welcome, Rob."

2   Use specific words to sound articulate.

My Dad pointed out how often we use the word, "basically." People who use the word "basically" sometimes use the word to "dumb down" the message for the listener, as if to imply that the listener couldn't possibly grasp the point if it were relayed in specific terms. "Basically" is an extraneous word in that it can be left out of most sentences without changing the meaning of the sentence. For example: Basically, this topic offers ideas on sounding intelligent.

3   Know what you're saying and they will, too.

It's fascinating how many people insert the question, "Do you know what I'm saying?" into their speech. The question, "Do you know what I'm saying?" suggests that the speaker doubts his own ability to communicate clearly. Self-doubt will not help you sound intelligent.

4   Edit your speech.

There are many words in the American English speech pattern that do not enrich the message or compliment the speaker. Years ago, John Lennon noted that the word "just" is an empty word that doesn't offer added meaning. Count how many times you hear the word "really" in a day. Also, listen for people to say, "you're kidding," in response to a person who obviously isn't.

5   Pause before speaking.

You can sound more intelligent by pausing a second or two before speaking. Former President Clinton was a master at hesitation. He would pause, hold up his relaxed fist, bite his lower lip and then speak. Clinton's pause was very effective because it helped him sound intelligent even when he was doing stupid things.

5 Cool Ideas™
for Your Elevator Speech

Imagine meeting someone on an elevator. Signals are exchanged and the other party is impressed enough to introduce himself or ask for your card. Of course, elevator speeches can be used in lots of places besides elevators. Brief and potent, these strong little impressions are made in 15 to 20 seconds. Trade these signals in dentist waiting rooms, restaurant foyers and business meetings. Elevator speeches can be used to introduce yourself to a stranger, to kick off a meeting and to greet a grocery store clerk. Use these potent impressions for dealing with difficult people, getting a job and psychologically moving others closer to you. Here are 5 Cool Ideas for your elevator speech.

1 Always stand when greeting someone.

When the other person is standing, this simple gesture establishes psychological equity and sets the stage for your elevator speech.

2 Your full name conveys personal power.

When introducing yourself, give your full name, especially if the other person has given you their full name. People who don't offer their name can be perceived as insecure or having low self-esteem. Saying your full name telegraphs personal power. Do not give your full name if it compromises your safety.

---

3 Shake hands as if you mean it.

I have several criteria for evaluating a handshake. I anticipate a firm grip, sustained eye contact and a pleasant expression. Amazingly, many people do not deliver in all three areas.

4 Tell people why they should be glad to see you.

Okay, you've got 15 seconds. Impress me. Tell me why you are unique. Don't tell me that you're married. That's not unique, lots of people are married. Tell me you love your wife and I'll be impressed. Avoid giving a job title that someone else gave you. In fact, avoid giving your title if it's not an exciting title.

5 You are judged by your signals.

Elevator speeches can be delivered in person, in e-mail signature files and in your outgoing voicemail message. See page 28 for *5 Cool Ideas for Your E-mail Signature File* and page 24 for *5 Cool Ideas for Effective Outgoing Voicemail*. The bottom line is this: if you send average signals, you are likely to be perceived as average. If you send exceptional signals, you are likely to be considered exceptional.

5 Cool Ideas™ for Better Feeling

5 Cool Ideas™
for Being Happy

Being happy seems like such a simple concept and yet, very few people are truly happy. My father reminded me of this in his letters. I read the letters in the audiobook, Dear Michael Angelo – A Father's Life Letters to His Son, which is available at www.EdisonHouse.com. In one of the letters, he wrote, "We want to be happier than other people, which is difficult since we believe them to be happier than they really are." Here are 5 Cool Ideas for being happier.

1 Accepting yourself can help you be happy.

My friend, Dr. Steve Fabick, is a psychologist. He says that being self-conscious can spoil almost any occasion. A man, for example, may not enjoy a fast dance with a woman because he can't stop thinking about how he looks. Many women are unable to relax if they are underdressed (or overdressed) for a dinner party. The key to accepting yourself is to be comfortable in any given situation without being held hostage by the need for self-improvement.

2 Make each day a "perfect" day.

List the things that make you happy. Be sure to include work and not just fun stuff. Your ultimate goal is to make sure that the activities on your list occur daily. When you can systemize these activities, every day will be a perfect day.

---

3 Helping others helps you.

Grievance counselors say that helping others is a terrific way to be happier. Create a tandem act of kindness. Distract yourself from problems by helping someone else. Years ago, I made a long-term commitment to Optimist International, Big Brothers/ Big Sisters and Rotary International, the largest professional service organization in the world.

4 Use the "reversal" to get a grip.

Wrestling fans know about a move called the reversal. It's what happens when the victim on the bottom ends up being the victor on the top. If you blame someone else for your unhappiness, ask yourself, "How long am I willing to be unhappy?" Reversing the blame will gently force you to realize that you are responsible for your happiness.

5 Happiness is a process, not a place.

I once facilitated a meeting for a company whose management preached the famous business model "management-by-objective" or MBO. As I spent time with the employees, it became clear that the rank-and-file were disenchanted with the MBO process. One employee actually told me, "This management-by-objective thing must not be working. This is the fifth year that we're doing it!" Management-by-objective is a process, not a place. The same is true for the management of emotions. The search for happiness requires lifelong dedication to patience, acceptance and planning.

5 Cool Ideas™
for Being Healthy

Do you know people who never seem to get sick? Colds and flu can be avoided with a strong immune system, a little luck and application of the following advice from the American Medical Association. Here are 5 Cool Ideas for being healthy.

1   Preventive measures can make your day.

Wine tasters tell us that dirty glasses can spoil a good wine. Think what dirty glasses and silverware can do to your health. Wipe off questionable utensils and the tops of soda cans before putting them to your mouth. Use paper towels to touch doors when exiting restrooms.

2   Water minimizes fatigue and germ entry.

Lack of water is a common source of afternoon fatigue. Drinking lots of water can also help a sore back, clear up your skin and help prevent urinary tract infections. Germs can enter through cracks in mucous membranes. Membranes are less likely to allow germs to enter when they are kept moist by the intake of six 8-ounce glasses of water per day.

3   Don't avoid Mr. Sandman, he's your friend.

Americans are notorious for not getting enough rest. This is especially surprising when you consider that most of us are watching extra television instead of getting extra sleep. If you're going to cheat Mr. Sandman, at least do something productive. Better still, get seven to eight hours of good quality sleep. Sleep allows your body to fight the good fight in warding off daytime drowsiness and anxiety. Adequate sleep also buoys your immune system.

4 Clean hands promote good health.

It's little wonder people are sick all the time. It's common to see people licking their fingers to count money. Watch people hold escalator handrails and then rub their eyes. You don't want to know how many men leave public restrooms without washing their hands. Let's review: John's hands get dirty. John touches face. John gets sick.

5 Antibiotics don't fight viruses.

There are two basic types of infections: bacterial and viral. Simply put, bacterial infections get better with antibiotics, while viral infections get better with time – time, cleanliness, rest, lots of water and preventive maintenance . . .

5 Cool Ideas™
for Healthy Travel

If being healthy at home is a treat, then being healthy on the road is a luxury. Each year I fly about 100,000 miles. Every year I rent about four dozen cars and sleep in 180 strange beds. I'll stay in a lot of hotels, too. Despite my incessant travel schedule, I rarely get colds and feel good almost every day. Here are 5 Cool Ideas for healthy travel.

1 Avoid sleeping with the enemy.

Towels and linens get washed daily, but bedspreads get laundered much less frequently. Bedspreads often provide a home to bacteria, dust mites and other undesirable bed mates. Anyone who lounges on hotel bed covers is inviting problems.

2 Airplane rides cause dehydration.

Hydration serves you especially well if you're 3,000 feet or more above sea level for an extended period of time. Most commercial airplanes fly at about 30,000 feet with cabins pressurized to about 8,000 feet. Bottled water can be a healthy constant for you when air quality and air pressure are in flux.

3 Use the shower to humidify the hotel room.

During dry winter months, run hot water through the hotel room shower head to humidify the room and put some much needed moisture in the air. I often run the shower while I unpack.

4   Wash your hands at least ten times per day.

Many people infect themselves by not keeping their hands clean. Avoid rubbing your eyes and putting your fingers near your mouth. Wash your hands with hot, soapy water every time you return from a public place.

5   Healthy thoughts are an advantage.

Say or think "I get sick every February" or "I'm catching a cold" and you could be coaching yourself into ill health. In some cases, you think you're catching a cold because you have cold symptoms, but the symptoms actually indicate that the malady is leaving your system. In reality, you're not "catching a cold," you're getting over one – unless your brain is behind the times. Eat safely on the road by visiting established restaurants with good reputations. Avoid purchasing food from dubious street vendors. Take some bismuth when in doubt about water and food quality. The bismuth will kill low-grade bacteria and give your digestive tract a fighting chance.

5 Cool Ideas™
for Better Sleep

In doing over 1,000 personal development seminars, I've asked a lot of people about their challenges. "I want to get more sleep," is a common response. Well, the secret to getting more sleep is to go to bed earlier. Let's dig a little deeper and discover why good sleep is important, how to prepare for quality sleep and how not to sleep. Here are 5 Cool Ideas for getting better sleep.

1 A lack of sleep can kill you.

According to the National Institute of Health, more than 70 million Americans have a sleeping problem. The annual economic cost of these problems amounts to billions of dollars in lost productivity. Here's something else to consider. The National Highway Traffic Safety Administration estimates that 56,000 accidents occur each year due to drivers who are asleep at the wheel.

2 A systematic wind down aids sleep.

To get better sleep, it helps to systematically unwind in the hours before bed. For example, I try not to eat after 7 p.m. and I don't answer e-mail or voicemail after 8 p.m. I don't deal with challenging thoughts or discussion after 9 p.m. Try to go to bed at about the same time every night. For more information on my wind down routine, access the toolbox at www.EdisonHouse.com.

---

3 You should only do two things in bed.

Sleeping is one of them. Reading, talking and eating in bed are bad habits because they distract the mind from peaceful rest.

4 Endorphins are a natural sedative.

I use endorphins to help me fall asleep. I smile, think a good thought and I go right to sleep almost every night. I often demonstrate my sleeping technique in seminars. After watching me stand in front of the class sighing, smiling and pretending to nod off, a gentleman raised his hand and shouted, "I can't smile before going to sleep. I'm married!" Smiling releases a natural painkiller called endorphins. It has been clinically proven that humans can release endorphins by "fake" smiling. Try it for 21 consecutive nights and send me a success story. Try it even if you're married.

5 Good sleep requires good sleep hygiene.

Many adults have learned how *not* to go to sleep. Poor sleep hygiene can keep you from obtaining quality sleep. It's important to have a clean, dust-free bedroom. Your mattress should be less than four years old and your bed linens should be laundered at least once a week. Make sure that your bedroom is dark and quiet when you go to sleep. Sweet dreams.

5 Cool Ideas™
for Reducing Stress

Experts have never identified stress as a direct cause of death, but the medical community almost unanimously agrees that stress can be deadly when combined with obesity, heart disease, smoking, depression and other serious health issues. In a long-term study of University of North Carolina alumni, people with high stress scores were more likely to die of heart attacks. Nearly 14 percent of those with high stress died in the 25 years following the test. Only 2 percent of people with low stress scores suffered heart attacks. Here are 5 Cool Ideas for reducing stress and possibly avoiding a heart attack.

1 You can refuse delivery on stress.

Since much stress is based in fear, you can give yourself a boost anytime, anywhere, by dealing with your fear. Metaphorically, spread your arms parallel to the ground and repeat the mantra, "You can't hurt me." The advanced version is "You won't hurt me. I trust you not to hurt me." Consult my booklet, *Hmmm...Little Ideas With BIG Results*, if you would like more information on this effective technique. It's available at www.EdisonHouse.com.

2 Learn how others deal with stress.

Pay attention to how people deal with bad news, long lines and disappointing service. Observe how some people respond to stress with aggression, anger and physical manifestation of their discomfort. Observe how other people respond to stress by smiling and asserting themselves without raising their voices. The second group of people have learned how to resist daily wear and tear on their emotions. Model this behavior and you will have less stress.

3 Say "so long" to negative people.

You have a limited amount of time to spend with others. Each hour you spend with negative people is an hour you can't spend with positive people. If you can't say "so long" to negative friends and associates, at least don't say "hello" as often.

4 Impose deadlines on stress.

Be proactive about stress by refusing to let it linger. If you're uptight about missing work after your surgery next month, promise yourself to start feeling better within a certain number of days after the operation. Here's another way to impose a deadline on stress. When someone yells at you, convince yourself that your anger need only be present until the person's words dissipate.

5 Repeat after me, "Mondays are good."

Many people don't like Mondays. They subscribe to the pervasive theory that the first business day of the week is going to be bad news. This is a depressing way to approach one-seventh of your life! Try thinking of Mondays as a fresh start to the week or the first day of the week that generates income. Over time, I've been able to convince myself that Monday is the best day of the week.

5 Cool Ideas™
for Guaranteed Vitality

The Merriam-Webster dictionary defines "vitality" as "the capacity to live and develop." Yet, many of us are content to live without developing. Some people would rather be on the sidelines than play the game. John F. Kennedy once observed that Americans seem to believe that attending a sporting event is similar to participating in the event. Our lives can be much richer when we actively participate. Here are 5 Cool Ideas for guaranteed vitality.

1   Play music, don't just listen to it.
Creating music on a piano or guitar is truly a magical experience. Original music is a gift for whoever is performing and a gift for whoever is listening. Singing is such a beautiful experience, yet many people never learn to carry a tune or to express themselves through song. When my brothers and I were young men, we toured the country in a rock band. The four of us played ten instruments including guitars, woodwinds, brass instruments, keyboards and percussion. Playing music is a lifelong joy for us. It's the gift that keeps on giving.

2   Learn to cook food, not just heat it.
In an age of instant gratification, we tend to buy food that is wrapped in cellophane and microwavable. Preparing food without a microwave is a rewarding experience. A good, home cooked meal can revitalize almost anyone. In any case, fresh, unprocessed food is certainly better for you.

---

3 Give presentations, don't just attend them.

A key to vitality is developing original ideas and sharing them with others. While everyone has something to say, few of us are willing to develop our speaking skills. Rather than develop and deliver a message, most people are content to sit in the audience while someone else shares ideas.

4 Write books, don't just read them.

How many times have you heard someone say "I should write a book?" How many times have you said this? While almost everyone can write something worthwhile, very few of us do. Because this is true, books don't get written, articles don't get published and letters don't get sent.

5 Participation guarantees vitality.

Celebrity worship is alive and well. People have come to believe that famous people are somehow more interesting than the rest of population. This is not necessarily true. I think *you* should move into the spotlight. Play some music while you cook dinner. Say something that draws a crowd and then write about the experience.

5 Cool Ideas™
for Maintaining Your Body Weight

I'm not an expert on losing weight, but having tipped the scales at about 163 pounds for the last 22 years, I've got some thoughts on how to stay fit and trim. Here are 5 Cool Ideas to maintain your body weight.

1 Order salad dressing on the side.

Never let a total stranger determine how much dressing will be on your salad. Always order dressing on the side and try not to use all the dressing they bring you. Never pour salad dressing directly onto your greens. At informal meals, dip your empty fork into your small dressing container, then spear some vegetables. At formal meals, spoon a little dressing onto a small area of your salad plate. Lightly dip the lettuce into the calories and you're more likely to maintain your body weight.

2 Do crunches while watching TV.

Weight shows up on the gut first. Work the gut first. Do your crunches every day, without fail. Do them first thing in the morning to get them over with. Keep an exercise mat in your television room and do crunches during the commercials of your favorite TV show.

---

3   Don't buy potato chips.

A big part of maintaining my body weight is winning
the head game. I've got a terrific technique for stay-
ing away from potato chips. I don't buy them. I
only order a restaurant dessert if I'll be sharing it.
If cookies come four to a pack, I'll eat two today
and two tomorrow in an effort to time-release those
fat grams.

4   Walking fast is the perfect exercise.

Walking fast can tone your backside, save time and
provide good cardiovascular exercise. Most of us
casually saunter from the car into the office, from
the airplane into the terminal and from the mall to
the car. Would you be willing to walk faster if it
helped keep your weight down? Try it for six months,
then send me a success story.

5   You should perspire when you exercise.

If your doctor gives you the okay, make time for 30
minutes of vigorous exercise at least three times per
week. If you're not perspiring during your workout,
you're probably not doing it right. Perspiration is an
indicator that your heart rate is elevated enough to
obtain the maximum benefits of exercise.

5 Cool Ideas™
for Losing a Headache

According to the National Headache Foundation, over 45 million Americans get chronic, recurring headaches. Industry loses $50 billion a year due to absenteeism and medical expenses related to headaches. More than $4 billion are spent annually on over-the-counter pain relievers, many of which are ineffective for the chronic headache sufferer. Here are 5 Cool Ideas for losing a headache.

1 Get your head checked.

There are two main types of headaches. The first type is the tension stress headache, which accounts for 90% of all headaches. Tension headaches can be episodic or daily occurrences. Daily headaches tend to be caused by depression and other emotional problems. The second main type of headache is the vascular headache, which includes migraines and cluster headaches. Most victims of cluster headaches are male. The cause of cluster headaches is unknown, but they can be controlled with treatment. Consult a physician if you have vascular headaches or if your headaches occur daily.

2 A water chaser can minimize hangovers.

Hangover headaches are often described as a throbbing, pounding pain accompanied by queasiness. Alcohol dilates blood vessels, which isn't a good thing. To counter the dehydrating effects of alcohol, take two aspirin with a good amount of water before bed. Drink more water and fruit juice in the morning.

---

3 Some headaches require a second opinion.

Pain radiating along the sides of the head, and jaw pain, can be a temporomandibular joint (TMJ) headache. With TMJ, there can be a distinct clicking upon opening or closing of the jaw. Movement may be limited. TMJ is caused by jaw misalignment. Sufferers can get relief by wearing an oral appliance. TMJ is often misdiagnosed, so get a second opinion.

4 Heat soothes raging sinus headaches.

Sinus headaches are evidenced by pain behind and below the eyes. Sinus headaches are sometimes accompanied by fever and facial swelling. Visit a doctor if you have fever or swelling. Otherwise, try hot compresses, steam, hot drinks and over-the-counter decongestants.

5 Migraine "activators" offer clues.

Migraines cause mild to severe throbbing on one side of the head accompanied by nausea, vomiting and sensitivity to light and noise. Migraines are hereditary and usually have triggers or activators like stress, menstruation, chocolate and red wine. People prone to migraines sometimes get headaches from activators such as sex, the food additive MSG and irregular living patterns. Your physician may ask you to keep a headache diary to help discover your migraine activators.

5 Cool Ideas™
for Getting More Sex

Here's an interesting observation. Almost all of my male friends would like to have more sex. They are the same men who tell me that while they are making love, they wonder when they'll be having sex again. Below are 5 Cool Ideas for getting more sex. Note: If you never feel sexually satisfied, you may have an addiction and should consult an addiction specialist.

1 Earn sex by showing respect.

It's been said that women give sex to get love and men give love to get sex. The truth is that you should give love to get love. Sex is a by-product of other life activities like communication, compassion and compromise. You can earn more sex by showing respect for the opposite gender. Learn to deliver deep compliments to your potential liaison.

2 Cleanliness is next to sexiness.

It seems obvious, but some people still don't get it. Bathe daily and use deodorant soap. The soap wrapper should display the word, "deodorant." Only use a deodorant whose package advertises "antiperspirant, deodorant." Regular flossing of the teeth is a great way to ensure fresher breath. Mouthwash works best when your mouth is really clean.

3   Details should be in your game plan.
Small gifts work wonders in earning you some quality time with your mate. Etiquette is important, too. Gentlemen, stand to greet a lady and smile more often. Ladies, speak up and be more assertive.

4   The chase is supposed to be fun.
Healthy sexuality has no place for inhibitions, fear, guilt or shame. Lose your baggage. Sex should be natural, easy and fun. Use music, candles and hot baths to help set the scene.

5   Mutual appreciation is a common bond.
Bonds are primarily established through communication, which means that you could enjoy more sex if you were a better listener. It would help if you were more articulate, too. Listen to subtle verbal cues and study nonverbal signals as if your lovemaking depended on it. See page 58 for *5 Cool Ideas for Better Listening.* Play the "Like Best" game with your mate. Take turns telling what you like about each other. Everyone loves to be appreciated. Using appreciation to establish a common bond is a great way to arrange for more sex.

5 Cool Ideas™
about You and the Apple

The apple has almost always been a part of human culture. First domesticated in Asia Minor, apples spread to eastern Europe. Greek and Roman mythology referred to the apple as a symbol for love and beauty. Early colonists brought apples to North America where they were grown as early as 1630. Shape magazine contributes some nutritional information about apples, the perfect food. Here are 5 of their coolest ideas.

1 Apples are perfectly good for you.

In many ways, apples are the perfect food. A medium-size apple has 5 grams of fiber and 20 grams of carbohydrates. It has virtually no fat or sodium and just 60-100 calories. Older people love apples. The "Granny Smith" apple was named after an elderly Australian woman named Maria Anne Smith.

2 Apples are healthy and delicious, too.

An apple's fiber, pectin and antioxidants can lower your LDL (the bad cholesterol) and raise your HDL (the good cholesterol). Apples are delicious, too. The "Delicious" apple was named when a fruit show judge bit into an apple submitted by a Quaker farmer named Jesse Hiatt. "Delicious!" the judge said.

3   Apples protect your teeth and eyes.

Everyone knows an apple a day keeps the doctor away. Apparently, an apple a day keeps the dentist away, too. The tannins in apples, prevent tooth decay and gum disease. An apple's vitamins may prevent age-related vision problems. William Tell must have eaten an apple before he used a bow and arrow to shoot an apple off his son's head. Not many people know that Tell did this at the rude insistence of invaders to Switzerland.

4   Apples can help extend your life.

An apple's flavonoids and other phytochemicals help guard against lung cancer. Apples contain boron, a mineral that helps maintain bone density and protect against heart disease. Heart disease is the leading cause of death in America. Homer, who died before he could visit America, refers to apples in *The Odyssey*, which was written between 900 and 800 B.C.

5   An apple is a gift that keeps giving.

Eating an apple a day may not completely keep the doctor away, but it can guard against stroke. The fruit has a flavonoid called quercetin, which may fight cancer better than vitamin C does. An apple's folic acid and vitamin B helps prevent serious birth defects. John Chapman, also known as Johnny Appleseed, gave apples to American pioneers as he traveled through the Ohio Valley in the first half of the nineteenth century.

5 Cool Ideas™
for Your Signature Story

Signature stories are short, personal narratives that help people relate to you. These narratives are usually upbeat tales that inspire and educate. Here are 5 Cool Ideas for your signature story.

1 Your story should be unique to you.

No one else can tell your signature story. It just wouldn't sound right coming from them. Be familiar and proud of your story. I have actually scripted a couple of my signature narratives. The scripts have been refined through the years and my signature stories are now quite polished. Many of my audiences have heard the story of how my Dad taught me self-esteem and how I practice my word-of-the-day. I have another story about a lesson learned when my Mom died.

2 Short stories have more impact.

Your signature story should be short and succinct, ideally less than five minutes. A short story will hold everyone's attention. This is important because signature stories should be told in a variety of settings. Even short stories have a beginning, a middle and an end. Short stories have plots, subplots and character development. The trick is to make every word count. Delete whatever doesn't contribute to the story.

---

3 Offer a lesson and people will listen.

Good signature stories offer a lesson. No one wants to hear how you went bankrupt and sunk into mental depression – unless you tell them how you emotionally recovered and became financially stable again. The story might illustrate how you lost 40 pounds or how you successfully managed a career transition. You might tell how you paid off a debt or otherwise delivered yourself from adversity.

4 Everyone loves a happy ending.

The ending of your signature story should be upbeat. Signature stories have a positive moral. As the storyteller, you become a living, breathing example of how good triumphs over evil.

5 Develop several signature stories.

Develop a personal story that teaches something about health. Have a good story about how you dealt with a difficult person and they turned out to be a good friend. Develop a story on how you transitioned your career or how you handled a challenging problem. Click the toolbox at www.EdisonHouse.com to read examples of my signature stories.

5 Cool Ideas™
about Exercise

Most people don't think about the serious issue of exercise until it's too late. Strength training, stretching, maintaining ideal body weight and breathing aren't usually top-of-mind issues, yet muscles, flexibility, mobility and cardio endurance sure come in handy when you're chasing the dog around the neighborhood. Here are 5 Cool Ideas for getting exercise into your life.

1 Exercise is a mindset, not an activity.

Welcome exercise into your life by thinking about it, then doing it. The trick to getting good exercise is to incorporate the concept into your thinking and to integrate the activity into your schedule.

2 Strength and endurance gives you new life.

Muscular endurance is defined by how long you can hold a position or repeat a movement. Muscular strength is defined by your ability to lift the heaviest weight you can, one time. Working out your abs may protect against diseases related to insulin resistance, such as diabetes and heart disease.

3 Stretching is a form of exercise.

Flexibility training promotes relaxation, improves performance and posture, reduces stress and keeps your body agile. Flexibility is a joint's ability to move through a full range of motion. A lack of flexibility could be an invitation to muscle tears and pulls. One form of flexibility training is called static stretching,

---

which involves gradual, controlled elongation of the muscle. After walking to warm up your large muscle groups, slowly stretch and hold still for 15-30 seconds in the furthest comfortable position. Never do bouncing, ballistic stretching, which violently pulls muscles.

4 Evaluate body composition, not weight.

Studies show that a typical person living in the western world loses muscle mass and gains fat starting at age 20. This is when weight gain begins for most people. Evaluate body composition rather than body weight. Body composition is the proportion of fat compared to bone and muscle. Your goal should be to have a healthy percentage of muscle and fat in your body. Your bathroom scale will *not* show the most important results of a diet because the scale does not indicate body fat or lean muscle mass. Consult a physician to learn your ideal body fat percentage. Do not use height-to-weight tables, body mass indexes or girth measurements to calculate body fat. The best way to monitor body fat is by measuring skinfolds, hydrostatic weighing or using Bioelectrical Impedance Analysis using a body fat scale.

5 Cardio endurance gives the breath of life.

Fitness programs increase your confidence and decrease your apprehension, thereby reducing your overall muscle tension. As exercise, walking can give you better health, fitness and attitude. If you walk incorrectly, however, you can waste time and risk injury. When walking, avoid the common mistakes of overstriding, slapping your feet on the ground, not bending your arms, leaning and not walking for at least 30 minutes. Now take a hike.

5 Cool Ideas™
for Your Power Hour

The first hour of the day sets the tone for the rest of the day. This is your time to program yourself for success and to get motivated for all you need to do. Your Power Hour may have to happen early. If the kids get up early, 6 a.m. may be their hour, which makes your Power Hour 5 a.m. Be very selfish about how you spend the first 60 minutes of your day. I've refined my Power Hour through the years and have been teaching it in seminars for a long time. Here are 5 Cool Ideas for your power hour.

1   In the morning, no news is good news.

Wake to music, rather than the alarm clock. Set the clock radio to awaken you at five minutes before the top or bottom of the hour so that you wake up to upbeat music, rather than negative news reports. Some CD players can be programmed to awaken you, which means you can awaken to your theme song every day. You do have a theme song, don't you? Also, do not read the newspaper during your Power Hour.

2   Self-affirmation is corny, but effective.

Every morning, I turn off the music, enjoy a deep sigh, a smile and a positive belief. The deep sigh rushes oxygen into my brain, which has been in a shallow breathing pattern all night. The smile releases endorphins, nature's pain killers. A positive belief such as "people want to meet me today," motivates me to get out of bed.

---

3   Wake up body parts separately.

To wake up my sleepy muscles, I stretch out on the floor to do 40 push ups and 100 stomach crunches. This takes about five minutes, but it's five minutes more exercise than some people get in a week. In the bathroom, I shower, shave and sing. I sing to wake up the right side of my brain and some of my neighbors. To awaken my left brain, I will read something motivational or write something that helps me feel good about myself.

4   Eat a vegetable at breakfast.

During my Power Hour, I eat a full breakfast, including three of the four major food groups. For me, breakfast includes some protein, a couple types of fruit and at least one vegetable. I drink a pint of water during my Power Hour to flush my system and replenish fluids. I always leave on time for my first appointment because leaving late sets up a negative domino effect that creates anxiety.

5   Early to bed means early to rise.

When getting ready for bed, no news is good news. I don't read the newspaper, watch or listen to the news after 7 p.m. because troubling headlines may keep me from sleeping. As a weight control method, I don't usually eat after 7 p.m., but if I must eat late, I try not to eat a whole beefsteak or something that's going to moooove around on me during the night. I don't answer the telephone after 8 p.m. because people who call that late are trying to provoke me. Late night callers want me to laugh, cry or think, none of which have anything to do with sleeping. When I go to bed, I smile, breathe a deep sigh and generate a positive belief. These techniques help me relax. I go to sleep within about five minutes every night.

5 Cool Ideas™
for Creating Reward/Consequence Proposals

Reward/Consequence proposals are a terrific way to influence others to do what you want them to do. Giving people a choice between reward and negative consequence allows them to make decisions that benefit everyone. The challenge is to communicate the reward and consequence with absolute clarity. Here are 5 Cool Ideas for reward/consequence proposals.

1 "I" statements cannot be denied.

"I" statements are an effective way to deliver a message because they immediately establish an agenda that cannot be denied. "I have a problem" and "I'm uncomfortable with this" are examples of "I" statements. "I" statements invite responses like "What is it?" and "How can I help?" "You" statements, on the other hand, can trigger anger and aggression. "You have a problem" is an example of a "you" statement.

2 Documentation is your friend.

When setting up a reward/consequence scenario, try to reference official documentation such as a report or some other statistical reference. This will strengthen your case and help the other person understand that it is not your word against his. Of course, the report is evidence, but you don't have to use that word. If the other person tries to discredit the report, ask them if they have a report for you to consider. When they answer, "no," say, "Then, let's consider this report for now." Link the other person's poor performance or misbehavior to the report.

3 Use a "call back" to stay on your agenda.

When confronted, people will sometimes try to distract you from the topic at hand. Casey McNeal, a friend and former stand-up comedian, taught me a technique referred to as a "call back." The "call back" is a terrific way to get others to focus on your agenda. When the other person tries to move the discussion off center, simply say, "You may be right, but I still have a problem." A firm return to your initial "I" statement allows very little sway in the conversation and keeps the focus on your agenda.

4 Empower others with a "proposal."

Use a reward/consequence proposal when both of the proposal's options move you toward your solution. After presenting the other person their two choices, say "Whatever you decide is okay with me." If you're thinking ahead, you can be sure that whatever option is chosen, things will work out for everyone.

5 You never win, you just keep playing.

Follow up is important when you use the reward/consequence scenario. Use language like "Let's meet again in two weeks" and "I see you've made a decision." Refer to "progress updates," not "deadlines." Remember, you never get to win the reward/consequence game, you just get to keep playing.

Index

Dear Michael Angelo

A Father's Life Letters to His Son

An audiobook by Michael Angelo Caruso, read by the author

My dad, Mickey Caruso, wrote over fifty letters between 1993 and 1997. These missives include dozens of vignettes that tell how his parents immigrated to the United States, what it was like to grow up during the Depression, how music impacted his life and what it was like to grow up with eleven brothers and sisters. These letters became a retroactive diary that chronicled the best of his life and taught me the value of keeping a journal to document life changes.

In the summer of 1997, my Dad and I talked about publishing his letters, but on September 24, our family changed again. As another chapter played out, the value of the written word became apparent...and yet another lesson was handed down from my father. Dad and I missed our opportunity to work together on this project, but my brothers and I know that he would want you to enjoy the world according to Mick. Dad's letters were a method of passing the benefits of his life lessons on to his family. With each person who experiences these letters, Mickey's family grows.

What people are saying:

"I listened to Dear Michael Angelo *twice before I figured out that the letters are not about Michael and his Dad as much as they are about my Dad and me."*
– Brenda Geist, Ft. Belvoir, VA

"I listened to stories from Michael's Dad and immediately wrote to my sons."
– Marty Bostrom, Marysville, TN

"... stirred my soul. I've given it to my children to urge them to keep their communication and love open."
– Lou Seimer, Baltimore, MD

Hmmm...
Little Ideas With BIG Results
A booklet by Michael Angelo Caruso

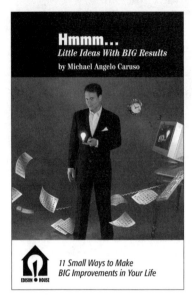

It's been fun creating this second edition of *Hmmm...Little Ideas With BIG Results*. The second edition is an improvement on the original version, thanks to feedback from hundreds of people who have published the Hmmms in corporate newsletters and thousands of audience members who have provided suggestions at my speeches and seminars.

The objective of this booklet is to help you discover new aspects of these simple thoughts and to encourage you to integrate them into your life. The Hmmms deal with fundamental life concepts – rough little diamonds that can be polished into increasingly valuable gems.

In these ways and others, the Hmmms will serve you the rest of your days.

What people are saying:

"A great combo of 'big picture' ideas. Immediately applicable!"
– Bethel Weiss, New York, NY

"Michael Caruso has put together an enlightening and motivational collection of wisdom sure to inspire the thinking of any progressive business leader."
– Marilyn Ross, author of *The Complete Guide to Self-Publishing*

"The simple truths that Michael taught me have enabled me to make drastic changes in my professional and personal life. I have become a change agent instead of a victim of change."
– Teresa Marquette, Washington, DC

www.EdisonHouse.com

MichaelCaruso@EdisonHouse.com

Books, Tapes & CDs | Calendar | Programs | Cool Ideas™ | Michael In Print
Rave Reviews | Guest Book | Contact Us

Michael's Calendar

Sunday	Monday	Tuesday	Wednesday	Thursday	Friday	Saturday
	Creativity Camp, Boston	Hero School, New York	Hmmm, DC	Talk to Me, Richmond	Talk to Me, Raleigh	

Programs

- Talk to Me (Conflict Resolution Made Easier)
- Customer Service (And What's In It For You)
- Creativity Camp
- Relationship Selling
- Hmmm
- Hero School

Gallery

Here, you can have fun with the people and events that have helped shape my life. Click on any picture to read the stories behind the images.

Michael Angelo Caruso In Print

Read articles published in
corporate newsletters and national publications.

Rooms: Home | Office | Souvenirs | Kitchen | Entertainment Center | Study | Gallery | Floor Plan
Subjects: Books, Tapes, CDs | Calendar | Programs | Cool Ideas™ | Michael in Print | Rave Reviews | Guestbook | Contact Us

www.EdisonHouse.com   143